Solution Focused Brief Therapy

Solution Focused Brief Therapy: 100 Key Points and Techniques provides a concise and jargon-free guide to the thinking and practice of this exciting approach which enables people to make changes in their lives quickly and effectively. It covers:

- the history and background to solution focused practice
- the philosophical underpinnings of the approach
- techniques and practices
- specific applications to work with children and adolescents (including schools-based work), families and adults
- how to deal with difficult situations
- organizational applications, including supervision, coaching, and leadership
- frequently asked questions

This book is an invaluable resource for all therapists and counsellors, whether in training or practice. It will also be essential for any professional whose job it is to help people make changes in their lives, and will therefore be of interest to social workers, probation officers, psychiatric staff, doctors, and teachers, as well as those working in organizations as coaches and managers.

Harvey Ratner, Evan George, and Chris Iveson founded BRIEF in London in 1989 as an independent training, therapy, coaching and consultation agency for the development of solution focused brief therapy.

100 Key Points

Series Editor: Windy Dryden

ALSO IN THIS SERIES:

Cognitive Therapy: 100 Key Points and Techniques
Michael Neenan and Windy Dryden

Rational Emotive Behaviour Therapy: 100 Key Points and Techniques
Windy Dryden and Michael Neenan

Family Therapy: 100 Key Points and Techniques
Mark Rivett and Eddy Street

Transactional Analysis: 100 Key Points and Techniques
Mark Widdowson

Person-Centred Therapy: 100 Key Points
Paul Wilkins

Gestalt Therapy: 100 Key Points and Techniques
Dave Mann

Integrative Therapy: 100 Key Points and Techniques
Maria Gilbert and Vanja Orlans

Solution Focused Brief Therapy: 100 Key Points and Techniques
Harvey Ratner, Evan George and Chris Iveson

Solution Focused Brief Therapy

100 Key Points and Techniques

*Harvey Ratner, Evan George,
and Chris Iveson*

 Routledge
Taylor & Francis Group

LONDON AND NEW YORK

First published 2012
by Routledge
27 Church Road, Hove, East Sussex BN3 2FA

Simultaneously published in the USA and Canada
by Routledge
711 Third Avenue, New York, NY 10017

*Routledge is an imprint of the Taylor & Francis Group, an Informa
business*

British Library Cataloguing in Publication Data
A catalogue record for this book is available from the British Library

Library of Congress Cataloging in Publication Data
Solution focused brief therapy : 100 key points and techniques /
Harvey Ratner, Evan George, Chris Iveson.
    p. cm. – (100 key points)
  ISBN 978-0-415-60612-7 (hardback) – ISBN 978-0-415-60613-4
(paperback) 1. Solution focused brief therapy.   I. Ratner,
Harvey.   II. George, Evan, 1951–   III. Iveson, Chris.
  RC489.S65S64 2012
  616.89'147 – dc23

                                    2011048157

ISBN: 978-0-415-60613-4 (pbk)
ISBN: 978-0-415-60612-7 (hbk)
ISBN: 978-0-203-11656-2 (ebk)

Typeset in Times New Roman
by RefineCatch Ltd., Bungay, Suffolk

Contents

Preface   x

Part 1   BACKGROUND   **1**
1   What is Solution Focused Brief Therapy?   3
2   The origins of Solution Focused Brief
     Therapy (1): Milton Erickson   6
3   Origins (2): family therapy and the Brief
     Therapy Center at the Mental Research
     Institute in Palo Alto   8
4   Origins (3): the Brief Family Therapy Center in
     Milwaukee and the birth of a new approach   10
5   The Brief Family Therapy Center: the first phase   12
6   The Brief Family Therapy Center: the second
     phase   14
7   Solution Focused Brief Therapy today   16
8   Philosophical underpinnings: constructivism   18
9   Philosophical underpinnings: Wittgenstein,
     language, and social constructionism   19
10   Assumptions in Solution Focused Brief Therapy   21
11   The client–therapist relationship   23
12   The evidence that Solution Focused
     Brief Therapy works   27

13 How brief is brief?   29
14 Summary: the structure of solution
    focused sessions   31

**Part 2 FEATURES OF SOLUTION
          FOCUSED INTERVIEWING   35**
15 Ideas about therapeutic conversation   37
16 Choosing the next question   38
17 Acknowledgement and possibility   40
18 Compliments   43
19 Deciding who to meet with   45

Part 3 GETTING STARTED   47
20 Problem-free talk   49
21 Identifying resources   52
22 Listening with a constructive ear: what the
    client *can* do, not what they cannot do   54
23 Constructive histories   56
24 Pre-meeting change   58

Part 4 ESTABLISHING A CONTRACT   61
25 Finding out the client's best hopes from
    the work   63
26 The 'contract': a joint project   65
27 The difference between outcome and process   67
28 The 'Great Instead'   70
29 When the client's hope is beyond the
    therapist's remit   72
30 When the client has been sent   74
31 Building a contract with young people   77
32 When the client says 'don't know'   79
33 When the client's hopes appear to be
    unrealistic   81
34 What if there is a situation of risk?   84
35 When the practitioner is a gatekeeper to
    a resource   86
36 What if we fail to develop a joint project?   89

Part 5   THE CLIENT'S PREFERRED FUTURE   91
37   Preferred futures: the 'Tomorrow Question'   93
38   Distant futures   95
39   The qualities of well-described preferred
      futures: the client's perspective   96
40   The qualities of well-described preferred
      futures: other person perspectives   98
41   Broadening and detailing   100

Part 6   WHEN HAS IT ALREADY HAPPENED?
           INSTANCES OF SUCCESS   103
42   Exceptions   105
43   Instances of the future already happening   107
44   Lists   109
45   No instances, no exceptions   112

Part 7   MEASURING PROGRESS: USING
           SCALE QUESTIONS   113
46   Scale questions: the evaluation of progress   115
47   Designating the '0' on the scale   117
48   Different scales   119
49   Successes in the past   121
50   What is good enough?   123
51   Moving up the scale   124
52   Signs or steps   125
53   What if the client says they are at '0'?   127
54   When the client's rating seems unrealistic   129

Part 8   COPING QUESTIONS: WHEN
           TIMES ARE TOUGH   131
55   Handling difficult situations, including
      bereavement   133
56   Stopping things from getting worse   135

Part 9 ENDING SESSIONS   **137**
57 Thinking pause   139
58 Acknowledgement and appreciation   141
59 Making suggestions   143
60 Making the next appointment   145

Part 10 CONDUCTING FOLLOW-UP SESSIONS   **147**
61 What is better?   149
62 Amplifying the progress made   150
63 Strategy questions   153
64 Identity questions   155
65 When the client says things are the same   157
66 When the client says things are worse   159

Part 11 ENDING THE WORK   **161**
67 Maintaining progress   163
68 What if there is no progress?   165

Part 12 ASSESSMENT AND SAFEGUARDING   **167**
69 Assessment   169
70 Safeguarding   171

Part 13 CHILDREN, FAMILIES, SCHOOLS, AND GROUPWORK   **173**
71 Children   175
72 Adolescents   177
73 Family work   179
74 Scales in family work   181
75 Couples work   182
76 In the school   185
77 Schools: individual work   187
78 Schools: the WOWW project   190
79 Groupwork   192

Part 14   WORK WITH ADULTS   **195**
  80   Homelessness   197
  81   Alzheimer's   199
  82   Learning difficulties   201
  83   Substance misuse   203
  84   Mental health   205
  85   Trauma and abuse   207

Part 15   SUPERVISION, COACHING, AND
             ORGANIZATIONAL APPLICATIONS   **211**
  86   Supervision   213
  87   Team supervision   215
  88   Coaching   217
  89   Mentoring   219
  90   Team coaching   222
  91   Leadership   224

Part 16   FREQUENTLY ASKED QUESTIONS   **227**
  92   Isn't it just a positive approach?   229
  93   Isn't it just papering over the cracks?   232
  94   It doesn't deal with emotions   234
  95   Isn't it just a strengths-based approach?   237
  96   What account does it take of culture?   239
  97   Isn't it just a form of problem-solving?   241
  98   It's a formulaic approach   243
  99   Can it be used with other approaches?   245
100   Self-help SFBT   247

  References   249

Preface

At the end of a third session at BRIEF during which the client had reported significant progress, the therapist asked whether any further sessions would be necessary. The client responded by saying:

> I don't feel I'm dependent on these meetings, which is a very good sign I think. I do feel I've changed. I have taken away some ideas about how to approach things. Some of the work we've done: it's very subtle, it's shifted things and helped a lot, and yet it seems quite simple in some ways, which is really lovely. I suppose it proves the point that you only have to make sometimes quite small adjustments that can have a very large impact on things, which is nice. I do like the fact that while there is the space here to discuss the background to things, not going over past things is actually quite good because that's a bit of an indulgence, it's quite nice to talk about the demons or whatever and sometimes that can help to take responsibility for the consequences of whatever, so I'm not saying that that kind of counselling isn't valid – I think it is – but I also think if someone's been traumatized they can be reliving that and that can almost make it worse in a way.

The client goes on to say how different the actual experience is from its description on BRIEF's website: a great deal more subtle.

So, in this book we will try to boil down Solution Focused Brief Therapy (SFBT) in a way that we hope will do justice to the richness of what is a subtle and intricate process. The solution focused approach is, undoubtedly, a radical approach, claiming that little or nothing needs to be known about the presenting problem (or what caused it) for the client to make good progress. Yet, at the end of the day, it's just a form of conversation. Steve de Shazer, one of the founders of the approach, was fond of repeating the story of when a receptionist at the Brief Family Therapy Center (BFTC) in Milwaukee asked to watch a session to see what it was all about. After a few minutes she said 'oh, it's all just a bunch of talk!', and went back to her desk in the reception area. But, as in the title of de Shazer's last book, 'words were originally magic' and a 'bunch of talk' is what creates the world and makes it go round.

BRIEF was established in 1989 by the three authors, all of whom are from social work backgrounds and are accredited family therapists. BRIEF is a therapy, coaching, training, and consultancy centre (www.brief.org.uk) with the largest training programme for brief therapy in the world. In this book, we will illustrate the techniques and ideas with examples taken from our own practice, all of which are, of course, altered in such as way as to protect the anonymity of clients. We would like to acknowledge the contribution made in recent years to our thinking by our former colleagues Yasmin Ajmal and Guy Shennan.

A word as to who this book is intended for. Many if not most of the approximately 70,000 practitioners who have attended BRIEF courses have not been working as 'therapists' or 'counsellors', and yet the solution focused approach is immensely useful to their work. As long as the practitioners concerned are working towards change with their clients, then there is a place for the therapeutic skills outlined in this book. Therefore, we believe that nurses, doctors, health advisers, teachers, mentors, social workers, probation officers, residential workers, foster parents, managers, and others will find much here that is relevant to their everyday work, as well as those working in more obvious 'change-oriented' ways such as therapists, counsellors, and coaches.

Part 1

BACKGROUND

1

What is Solution Focused Brief Therapy?

Solution Focused Brief Therapy (SFBT) is an approach to enabling people to build change in their lives in the shortest possible time. It believes that change comes from two principle sources: from encouraging people to describe their *preferred future* – what their lives will be like should the therapy be successful – and from detailing the skills and resources they have already demonstrated – those *instances of success* in the present and the past. From these descriptions, clients are able to make adjustments to what they do in their lives.

SFBT is a method for *talking* with clients. It holds the view that the way clients talk about their lives, the words and the language they use, can help them to make useful changes, and therefore SFBT is a language for, as one commentator put it, clients literally talking themselves out of their problems (Miller 1997: 214).

The BRIEF team, known initially as the Brief Therapy Practice, was the first team in the UK to practise SFBT. At that time, in the late 1980s, the approach seemed radically different. The idea that problems could be solved even when the therapist does not know the specifics of what is being complained about, and that clients 'have got what it takes', seemed naive to many. If we add to that the expectation that clients would only need an average of three to four sessions, the approach that emerged was an invitation to ridicule.

However, from the perspective of the second decade of the twenty-first century, many of the core tenets of the approach have long been taken up and adopted by other therapy approaches such that the distinctive features of the approach are no longer obvious. It has even been suggested that it is easier now to say what SFBT is *not* rather than what it is (McKergow and Korman 2009). For example, while practitioners of most approaches today will say they use future focused questions with their clients and may even use the so-called Miracle Question (regarded by many as the most famous invention of those who first devised the model), it is still usual for practitioners to say that they regard it as essential that clients be encouraged to talk about their problems at the outset and that the development of a problem formulation is an essential part of the process. Solution focused practitioners recognize that clients expect to be able to talk about their problems in therapy but do not *encourage* them to do so and often deliberately divert the client towards 'solution talk' (Berg and de Shazer 1993). Furthermore, some approaches will expect to end the session with the therapist providing the client with advice on what they should do next, or at least some sort of homework task for them to practise to solve their problem. While some solution focused therapists will give simple tasks to their clients, these are rarely more than asking a client to notice changes in their lives before the next session. There is an almost complete absence from the approach of giving advice. Insoo Kim Berg, one of the founders of the approach, was fond of advising therapists to 'leave no footprints in their clients' lives', meaning to intervene as little as possible and as *briefly* as possible. The 'intervention' is the interview itself, and nothing more.

In summary, SFBT is a time-sensitive approach to exploring with clients how they would like their lives to be as a result of the therapy, and examining the skills and resources they have for getting there. It is *not* about the therapist assessing the type of problem the client has and/or providing the solution to the client's problem. It has to come from the client.

Today, it is possible to talk of 'brief therapy approaches', approaches based on a variety of models as diverse as psycho-dynamic or cognitive behavioural therapy. The only connecting factor might seem to be the deliberate intention to intervene briefly – a pre-existing approach has been taken and ways found to deliver it in a more time-efficient manner.

However, there are also therapies originally designed to be brief. The Brief Therapy Center at the Mental Research Institute (MRI) in Palo Alto, California was established in 1967 with that express aim, and their clients are told at the outset that they will receive a maximum of ten sessions. The Brief Family Therapy Center (BFTC) was established in Milwaukee in 1977 as 'an MRI of the midwest' (Nunnally *et al.* 1985: 77), and from their own synthesis of the work of the MRI, the work of the hypnotherapist Milton Erickson, and family therapy methods, they came to develop SFBT. While they did not retain the ten-session limit of the MRI, they noted from their follow-up studies that by its very nature 'solution focused therapy' is brief. Subsequently, they stated that 'it is important to define brief therapy in terms other than time constraints because across the board clients tend to stay in therapy for only 6 to 10 sessions regardless of the therapist's plans or orientation. Therefore, we draw a distinction between (a) brief therapy defined by time constraints and (b) brief therapy defined as a way of solving human problems' (de Shazer *et al.* 1986: 207). The solution focused approach is, therefore, part of a particular brief therapy tradition with distinctive methods and philosophy.

2

The origins of Solution Focused Brief Therapy (1): Milton Erickson

Milton Erickson was a psychiatrist and hypnotherapist who died in 1980. Erickson wrote little about his work but has been the inspiration for many therapists and schools of therapy: Ericksonian hypnotherapy, neuro-linguistic programming (NLP), and many aspects of family therapy all owe much to Erickson who always claimed to have no theory.

Ericksonian stories abound but the best collection is to be found in Jay Haley's *Uncommon Therapy* (Haley 1973). The extent of his influence on SFBT can be seen in de Shazer's early writings. For example, he quotes Erickson as saying,

> in rendering him [the patient] aid, there should be full respect for and utilization of whatever the patient presents. Emphasis should be placed more on what the patient does in the present and will do in the future than on mere understanding of why some long-past event occurred. The sine qua non of psychotherapy should be the present and the future adjustment of the patient.
>
> (de Shazer 1985: 78)

de Shazer went on to describe Erickson's crystal ball technique, which encouraged clients, under hypnosis, to hallucinate the successful overcoming of their problems, and this was clearly a precursor to the 'Miracle Question' that invited clients to imagine 'life without the problem'. de Shazer commented that

> these ideas are utilized to create a therapy situation in which the patient could respond effectively psychologically to desired therapeutic goals *as actualities already achieved* . . . As I see it, the principles behind this [crystal ball] technique

form the foundation for therapy based on solutions rather than problems.

(de Shazer 1985: 81)

de Shazer noted that Erickson appeared to approach each patient with an expectation that change is not only possible but inevitable (1985: 78) and he linked this to Buddhist thought: change is a continual process and stability is only an illusion.

In summary, the elements of Erickson's practice that came to matter most to the development of brief therapy were:

- utilizing what the client brings
- non-normative (i.e. not prescriptive of what people should do)
- not interested in the client's past, or in developing insight
- crystal ball technique
- setting tasks
- therapist is responsible for success or failure of the therapy.

3

Origins (2): family therapy and the Brief Therapy Center at the Mental Research Institute in Palo Alto

The Mental Research Institute (MRI) was established by psychiatrist and early family therapist Don Jackson in 1959, and the Institute became famous for developing ideas and researching communication and therapy. In 1967, a centre was set up there to practise brief therapy, from which a new school of family therapy – strategic family therapy – was to emerge.

The team at the centre, led by John Weakland, Paul Watzlawick, and Dick Fisch, were interested in patterns of communication, particularly around problems, and notions to do with homeostasis that were thought to gauge how systems change or resist change. Their interest in the patterns of interaction around the identified client led to a novel view about problem formation:

> One of this group's most influential ideas was the notion that problems develop from and are maintained by the way that, under certain circumstances, particular, and often quite normal, life difficulties become perceived and subsequently tackled. Guided by reason, logic, tradition or 'common sense', various attempted solutions are applied (which can include a denial of the difficulty) which either have little or no effect or, alternatively, can exacerbate the situation [. . .] Therapy is focused on changing the 'attempted solutions', on stopping or even reversing the usual approach, however logical or correct it appears to be.
>
> (Cade 2007: 39–40)

Under Erickson's influence, the MRI team made no attempt to understand the problem and its 'underlying causes'. Instead, they accepted the problem at face value, looking at what was happening in the here and now around the problem and seeking to influence the client(s) to change their behaviour. They did not engage in formal hypnotic work but studied Erickson's use of language to learn how to frame tasks that would influence the client in the direction of change. For example, they would often suggest to clients that they 'go slow' in making changes (Weakland *et al.* 1974), telling them that, for example, now might not be the time to risk making changes that could, if anything, make matters worse; the paradoxical effect was often to spur the client on to make more changes. They developed the technique known as 'reframing', in which the problem or problematic behaviour is given a surprisingly different description to encourage the client to see herself in a different light (Watzlawick *et al.* 1974: 95). In an unusual case of a man who had a pronounced stammer and yet wanted to succeed as a salesman, his 'attempted solution' – trying to stammer less – was exacerbating the stress he felt and making things worse. They encouraged him to view his disability as an advantage, a way of capturing the attention of would-be customers who are put off by

> the usual fast, high-pressure sales talk . . . he was especially instructed to maintain a high level of stammering, even if in the course of his work, for reasons quite unknown to him, he should begin to feel a little more at ease and therefore less and less likely to stammer spontaneously.
>
> (Watzlawick *et al.* 1974: 94–95)

The MRI offered clients a maximum of ten sessions. If clients made sufficient progress in fewer than the ten, they could keep the remaining sessions 'in the bank' to draw on if needed in future. They reported excellent outcome figures for their work (Weakland *et al.* 1974).

4

Origins (3): the Brief Family Therapy Center in Milwaukee and the birth of a new approach

The story of SFBT starts, appropriately, with John Weakland at the MRI. He had befriended a young therapist and former saxophone player, Steve de Shazer, who was living in Palo Alto and had done some work at the MRI – it is probable that de Shazer did some training there. Weakland introduced de Shazer to another trainee, Insoo Kim Berg, and the pair married and decided to set up a brief therapy centre in de Shazer's home town of Milwaukee. In time, the pair gathered around them a team of talented and diverse therapists and researchers. In a footnote to an article, de Shazer (1989: 227) said of the title they gave their centre, 'what else could a group of therapists, half "brief" therapists and half "family" therapists, call their institute?' Although many of their early papers were published in the family therapy press, it is clear that de Shazer identified himself as a *brief* therapist and that the initial work of the team was very close to that of the MRI. In time, the sheer creativity of the group led to the development of new ideas, and they were also open to whatever thinking was fresh at the time, such as the work of Don Norum, a social worker in Milwaukee who wrote a paper (which was rejected by *Family Process* in 1979) called 'The Family has the Solution' (Norum 2000).

The early approach they used was oriented towards identifying the patterns of behaviour around the problem, and working out tasks that could be given to clients to influence them towards change. Attention was also paid to what would constitute minimal goals for therapy, and techniques such as the aforementioned crystal ball technique of Erickson (although used without hypnosis) were seen to raise 'expectations for a future without the complaint' (de Shazer 1985: 84). Akin to the family therapy technique of circular questioning, they adopted 'other person perspective' questions that invite the client to see themselves as others see them and to look at the impact of their changed behaviour on others and vice versa. The place of Erickson in their thinking is evidenced by their use of his ideas about utilization to find ways of developing cooperation with clients, and de Shazer proposed that a client's resistance be seen as the client's unique way of attempting to cooperate; in 1984, he brought this idea to fruition in a paper called 'The Death of Resistance'.

In the same paper, de Shazer referred to a task that the team had developed: 'between now and the next time we meet, we would like you to observe, so that you can describe to us next time, what happens in your family that you want to continue to have happen' (de Shazer 1984: 15). Elsewhere (DeJong and Berg 2008) we learn that it was when faced by a family who had listed 23 different family problems, and the therapy team didn't know where to start, that they decided to give this task. The result was that the family returned to report a number of things they had noticed and, moreover, some of these things seemed new to them, so they had made progress and didn't need further therapy. The team began experimenting with giving the same task to other clients, and found the same result. Consequently, in 1984, they undertook a research study in which therapists were asked to give this task, dubbed The First Session Formula Task (FSFT), to every client; the outcome was staggering. What was particularly impressive to the team was that it broke the 'rule' that the therapeutic task should be constructed to fit with the client's specific problem presentation. Instead, here was a generic task that was being given to clients regardless of the presenting problem. When de Shazer and Kim Berg presented on SFBT for the first time in London (presentation organized by BRIEF in 1990), de Shazer said that it was out of this task that the whole of the solution focused approach to brief therapy was developed. It led directly to the notion of 'exceptions to the rule', which, de Shazer suggested, are times when clients are overcoming their problems but 'these exceptions frequently slip by unnoticed because these differences are not seen as differences that make any difference: the difference is too small or too slow' (1985: 34). He explained that the FSFT was one among several tasks that they regarded as 'skeleton keys' (see Chapter 59 for more examples) that could unlock many problem locks; there was no need to find a different key for each problem.

5

The Brief Family Therapy Center: the first phase

In his first book *Patterns of Brief Family Therapy* (1982), de Shazer had insisted on the centrality of the observing team, whose job it was to assist the therapist (who acted as a conductor on behalf of the team) in the construction of an appropriate task, much as was practised at the MRI. Gradually, it had become clear that the therapist was not merely collecting information for the observers to use. The interview itself was seen to be therapeutic and by his second book (de Shazer 1985: 18) he was saying a team was 'stimulating but not necessary'.

Other techniques were being developed, most notably the use of 0 (or 1) to 10 rating scales to enable clients to define the degree of progress they were making towards their goals. de Shazer credited clients in the early 1970s with teaching him the use of these questions. Initially, he saw them as at their most useful with clients who were vague about their problems. The earlier MRI approach had emphasized the need for the therapist to be clear as to what the problem was and how it was being dealt with, so clients who were vague made this approach awkward, but with a scale the client could begin to define things by a number.

In *Keys*, de Shazer referred to William of Ockham, a fourteenth-century philosopher, who said that 'what can be done with fewer means is done in vain with many' (1985: 58). This principle, known as Ockham's Razor, became a central feature of the drive to find the minimum required to do effective therapy.

In this initial phase, 1982–1987, the solution focused model was based primarily on finding exceptions and helping clients to expand on them. The solution focused approach was formally announced to the world in the pages of *Family Process* in 1986 in an article entitled 'Brief therapy: focused solution development' (de Shazer *et al.* 1986), in a deliberate reference to the classic MRI paper 'Brief therapy: focused problem resolution', which had appeared in the same journal 12 years previously.

The team organized a project to look at pre-therapy change (Weiner-Davis *et al.* 1987), which found that when clients were asked to look out for changes *before* their first appointment, two-thirds reported that things had improved. What the team learned from this was that, for many clients, the change process is already happening, both before the first session and during it. The task of the therapist was therefore one where she needed to assist the change process rather than to start it, to amplify what was already happening. Referring to Buddhist thought, de Shazer said that change is constant, stability an illusion.

However, in his book *Becoming Miracle Workers* (1997), Gale Miller, a sociologist who observed the work of the Milwaukee team over many years, suggested that this phase constituted merely the first phase of the development of solution focused therapy, saying that strictly speaking it wasn't actually solution focused. He called it 'ecosystemic brief therapy', saying its predominant aim had been to define existing patterns of pathological communication and seek appropriate tasks for the family to perform so as to disrupt those patterns. For Miller, the turn to a truly solution focused orientation came with the development of what was to become known as the 'Miracle Question', which allowed clients to talk about their lives in new ways.

6

The Brief Family Therapy Center: the second phase

> Suppose one night there is a miracle. And the problems that brought you in here today are solved. OK? This happens while you're sleeping so you can't know it's happened. (client: 'OK') OK? The next day, how would you discover there'd been a miracle? What would be different that would tell you that a miracle has happened?
>
> (de Shazer 1994: 114)

Various stories were told about the origin of the Miracle Question. What is not in doubt is that it was first used by Insoo Kim Berg in the early 1980s but its significance was not appreciated for some years. It merited only a casual reference in the 'classic' paper of 1986, but within two years, in his book *Clues* (1988), de Shazer was heralding the question as the cornerstone of the solution focused approach.

At first the team saw the question as just another way to assist clients in defining their goals from the therapy. Gradually they realized that the responses they were getting from it were richer than those that they were accustomed to obtain. Clients were clearly using their imaginations to picture this event (in the way that Erickson had seen possible with his crystal balls technique) and rather than using the question to give unrealistic answers, it seemed that the question was enabling them to be realistic and to even appear to be having an experience of the after-miracle picture just from talking about it.

> Regularly – not every time the question is asked, but regularly – and more often with the increasing experience of the therapist, clients will behave as if they are experiencing what happens the day after the miracle. Clients will accompany the descriptions with bodily movements

as if they were doing and experiencing what they are describing.

(de Shazer et al. 2007: 40)

The procedure for a first session now became that after a client had been asked what brought them in, they were quickly asked to suppose that a miracle had solved that problem or problems. They were then asked to think of the most recent occasion they could remember when things were like the day after the miracle – exceptions or 'pieces of the miracle' (de Shazer 2001). Then they were asked to use a progress scale to figure out where they were in relation to their goals for therapy; the scale was subsequently described as 'The Miracle Scale' (de Shazer et al. 2007: 61).

The approach had therefore come a long way from just a few years before when, as at the MRI, the therapist was supposed to gather information that the observing team would use to construct a homework task for the client. Tasks became reduced to inviting clients to notice signs of the miracle happening, or even to *pretending* that the miracle had started to happen!

7

Solution Focused Brief Therapy today

The period from 1982 to 1994, between de Shazer's first single-authored book and his last, was a remarkable time of creativity and development in the world of brief therapy. From that point onwards, the team at BFTC in Milwaukee effectively disbanded and de Shazer gave his time increasingly to philosophical investigations. His wife Insoo Kim Berg, on the other hand, continued on a journey that had already begun with her book on working with families, *Family Preservation* (1991), and a joint work with Scott Miller on *Working with the Problem Drinker* (1992). What was interesting about these was that while conceptually they did not take the model any further forward, they nevertheless opened it up to its use in all manner of client services, given that agencies are usually established to meet defined client need. So while SFBT is assumed to be applicable to all clients regardless of their presenting problems, practitioners working in particular kinds of settings are eager to know how to apply the approach with their clients. In later years, Berg would go on to write books relating the model to child protection, to substance misuse, to work with children, to coaching, and, at the time of her death, was engaged on a book introducing a radical approach to work in schools (known as WOWW – see Chapter 78). She was famous for working to bring therapy out from the therapy room and into soup kitchens and streets where crucial front line work goes on.

In recent years, it has become common to refer to 'solution focused practice' rather than SFBT when the approach is used by non-therapists within other roles, such as coaching, mentoring, nursing, and social work. Furthermore, different versions of the approach are now in evidence, usually related to whether the practitioner has stayed close to the original model proposed in the mid-1980s by BFTC, or has taken on board new developments such as those instituted by teams like BRIEF; it is therefore possible to refer today to 'solution focused approaches'.

At BRIEF, we think of our work as a continuation of that of BFTC, in particular the application of the philosophical principle of which de Shazer was so fond, namely Ockham's Razor (whereby we aim for what is the minimum needed to be done in any given session), as well as the need to check consistency of outcomes from the client's point of view (Shennan and Iveson 2011). Accordingly, we have made some adjustments to the earlier model. For example, long before he died, de Shazer was aware that we were reducing the centrality of the Miracle Question in our work and that we very rarely gave homework tasks to clients. He accepted our reasons for this and welcomed our attempts to take the brief therapy tradition forward.

Since it was founded in 1989, BRIEF has been the largest provider of training in brief therapy in the world, with nearly 70,000 practitioners attending courses. Over time, SFBT has become an accepted method of practice in the UK – in 2010, the National Audit of Psychological Therapies conducted by the Royal College of Psychiatrists listed SFBT among the therapies being practised. British authors have contributed to the growing library of books and papers on the use of the approach in a range of settings. The United Kingdom Association for Solution Focused Practice (www.ukasfp.co.uk) was established in 2003. There are also associations in North America and in Europe and Australia and New Zealand. SFBT is well known in Singapore and Japan and Alasdair Macdonald and others from the UK have delivered training in China.

8

Philosophical underpinnings: constructivism

> The client is a different person after the Miracle Question than they were before.
>
> (presentation by Steve de Shazer to
> BRIEF in London, 1993)

Here, de Shazer was most likely speaking literally, because he was adopting a *constructivist* position, one based on the philosophical viewpoint that reality is invented rather than discovered; it involves a shift away from objectivism (de Shazer 1991: 46). This view is most controversial in relation to diagnosis in mental health. Much of psychological medicine up to the current time has been spent on attempting to define ever more closely the 'conditions' from which people suffer. This is based on structuralist thinking that there is a reality 'out there' (for example, 'depression') that can be defined and then treated. For post-structuralists such as practitioners of solution focused work, there is the worry that talk about, for example, depression, objectifies depression. Depression then becomes as much a reality, a given, for the client as is the fact they are male or female, white or black. Gale Miller argued that people talk themselves into problems and therapy is 'the process of talking clients out of their troubles' (Miller 1997: 214).

> It is not that we don't confront difficult problems in our lives, problems that are very real and often very painful. However . . . these realities are constructed; problems are not 'out there' as realities independent of us, but come to be what they are by virtue of the way we negotiate reality.
>
> (Gergen 1999: 170)

9

Philosophical underpinnings: Wittgenstein, language, and social constructionism

Ludwig Wittgenstein, a major philosophical influence, developed the notion of a 'language game', suggesting that words take on different meanings depending on the context in which they are used and the rules for using them. 'Following Wittgenstein, we can only know what a word means by how the participants in the conversation use it' (de Shazer 1991: 69). A problem focused language game is one such game, usually incorporating negative and past-history focused language that suggests the permanence of a problem. A solution focused language game, in contrast, is usually more positive, hopeful and future focused, and suggests the transience of problems (de Shazer *et al.* 2007: 3). A distinction was made between 'problem talk' and 'solution talk', in that 'problem talk belongs to the problem itself and is not part of the solution' (Berg and de Shazer 1993: 8). On the other hand, 'as client and therapist talk more and more about the solution they want to construct together, they come to believe in the truth or reality of what they are talking about. This is the way language works, naturally' (Berg and de Shazer 1993: 9). This linguistic approach has attracted criticism, including that it is overly intellectual and does not pay sufficient attention to people's emotions, against which de Shazer argued that emotions are a part of language and therefore clients are not prevented from talking about their emotions and, in any case, quoting Wittgenstein, 'an "inner process" stands in need of outward criteria' (de Shazer 1991: 74), hence the focus on behaviours in solution talk. A further criticism is that it does not pay sufficient attention to the social and political contexts of clients' lives, to which de Shazer argued that if the client wasn't mentioning external issues (such as bad housing, racism) for the therapist to do so was to bring their own political agenda into the therapy room (Miller and de Shazer 1998).

The predominant philosophical position that SFBT is closest to is *social constructionism*. 'Constructivism proposes that each individual mentally constructs the world of experience ... the process of world construction is psychological; it takes place "in the head". In contrast, for social constructionists what we take to be real is an outcome of social relationships' (Gergen 1999: 236–237). This means that when we construct the world we do so largely with categories supplied by social relationships. This explains the emphasis in solution focused therapy on asking questions about the client's relationships with others as well as with themselves. It also entails paying particular attention to the therapeutic relationship being developed, ensuring a cooperative relationship with clients. Rather than the therapist having the job of assessing and diagnosing the client so as to arrive at the correct advice or prescription, the client and therapist work *jointly* on the client's future. As de Shazer quipped (ascribing his joke to John Weakland), 'therapy is about two people trying to find out what the hell one of them wants!' This requires the therapist to accept that while therapists are experts on asking useful questions, they are not experts on clients' lives. If the client is to be trusted to know best what she wants in her life, then it follows that only *she* can judge the outcome of therapy: 'problems are resolved when clients' evaluations indicate that this is the case. This stance created some formidable distance between de Shazer and the evidence-based community, who distrust client feedback and evaluation as a sole source of knowledge' (Walsh 2010: 25).

One final point: de Shazer's post-structuralist view meant that he was against the notion that a *theory* could be developed that would explain how any therapy works. Instead, he used philosophy as a way to give 'light to description rather than explanation' (Simon and Nelson 2007: 156). Just as he would argue, when asked about other models of therapy, that he could only describe what he saw happening (rather than give a theory about it), so he would emphasize that when talking about clients one should only *describe* what one has seen and heard, avoiding all interpretation and in so asserting he followed Wittgenstein.

10

Assumptions in Solution Focused Brief Therapy

As de Shazer was fond of saying, SFBT has no theory base. But, as we have seen, there have been strong philosophical influences and it is certainly true that practitioners share a number of assumptions about clients and therapy.

1. All clients are motivated towards something. Clients do not lack motivation and it is the therapist's job to uncover what they are motivated towards.
2. It is the task of the worker to determine the client's unique way of attempting to cooperate with the work and thus to discover the best way to cooperate with the client's way of attempting to cooperate. The idea of 'resistance' is not a useful one, impeding the development of cooperation between the worker and the client.
3. Attempting to understand the cause of a problem is not a necessary or particularly useful step towards resolution. Indeed, sometimes discussing the problem can be actively unhelpful to clients.
4. Successful work depends on knowing what the client wants from the therapy. Once this is established, the task of therapy is to find the quickest way there.
5. However fixed the problem pattern may appear to be, there are always times when the client is doing some of the solution. The most economical approach to therapy involves helping the client do more of 'what already works'.
6. Problems do not represent underlying pathology. They are just things that the client wants to do without. In most cases, therefore, it is the client who will be the best judge of when the problem is resolved.
7. Sometimes only the smallest of changes is necessary to set in motion a solution to the problem. It is not invariably necessary to see everyone involved in the problem; in fact, it

is not always necessary even to see the person who is said to have the problem.

de Shazer referred to three rules, which, he said, 'form the underlying philosophy of brief therapy' (de Shazer 1989: 93):

1. If it ain't broke, don't fix it.
2. Once you know what works, do more of it.
3. If it doesn't work, don't do it again. Do something different.

In the last book to carry de Shazer's name, other 'major tenets' (de Shazer *et al.* 2007: 2–3) were added:

1. Small steps can lead to big changes.
2. The solution is not necessarily related to the problem.
3. The language for solution development is different from that needed to describe a problem.
4. No problem happens all the time; there are always exceptions that can be utilized.
5. The future is both created and negotiable.

11

The client–therapist relationship

In *Clues* (1988), de Shazer, adapting a classification from the MRI, denoted client–therapist relationships in three ways: customer, complainant, and visitor. This was connected to the idea that 'a therapeutic conversation can be punctuated as beginning with a complaint' (1988: 88). 'Sometimes people seem to have no complaints and their reason for being in the therapist's office is simply that someone told them to come or someone brought them' (1988: 87). Describing the relationship with this person as a visitor-type indicates the need to treat them as a visitor and not to impose therapy or tasks on them; instead, he recommended being complimentary, being on their side, and looking for what works rather than what doesn't. 'Complainant' describes a relationship where someone recognizes there is a problem but seems uninterested or unwilling to do anything about it. The rules in approaching them are similar to the visitor. It is only when someone actually wants to *do* something about their problem that the relationship can be said to be a customer-type.

By 1991 de Shazer's thinking had changed. In that year, BRIEF invited de Shazer and Berg to make a presentation under the title of 'Reluctant Clients'. However, midway through the event, de Shazer declared that there was no such thing as a reluctant client: everyone was a customer for something, even if it was to get someone else off their back. He had come to feel that the distinctions made just a few years earlier were a distraction, leading practitioners into thinking they have to assess the motivation of clients. Rather, if we take seriously what the client wants from meeting with us, even if it is not to have to meet us again, then this is the basis for a collaborative working relationship. At the heart of SFBT is cooperation with what the client wants.

In the following example, the therapist assumes that the client has come to the meeting (in a counselling room within a large secondary school) for a 'good reason'. The therapist implicitly includes his assumption in every question and eventually the same assumption is reflected in the client's answers.

Therapist:	Jessica, what are your best hopes from this meeting?
Jessica:	I have no idea and to be honest I haven't given it much thought.
Therapist:	So thinking about it now, what *are* your best hopes from this meeting?
Jessica:	I don't really have any.
Therapist:	And if it turned out to be useful what do you hope it might lead to?
Jessica:	I don't think it will be useful; these meetings never are.
Therapist:	Okay, so it's not your idea of a good idea?
Jessica:	No, not really.
Therapist:	Yet here you are – how come?
Jessica:	I didn't have any choice, I was told I had to come.
Therapist:	That's hard because I'm getting the idea that you are a pretty strong-minded person and probably like to make your own decisions. Would that be right?
Jessica:	Sometimes.
Therapist:	So how come you decided to cooperate and come along here?
Jessica:	Like I said, I didn't have a choice.
Therapist:	I can't imagine that you always do as you are told!
Jessica:	No.
Therapist:	How come you decided to do as you were told on this occasion?
Jessica:	Because I'll get excluded if I don't.
Therapist:	Okay, so, if possible, you need to find a way to stay in school, at least for now?
Jessica:	Yes.
Therapist:	So if this meeting somehow helps you to find a way to stay in school that is right for you as

> well as right for the school, will that mean it
> has been useful?
>
> *Jessica*: I suppose so.
> *Therapist*: Okay. Can I ask you some questions?
> *Jessica*: Go on then.

Whether Jessica actually had a good reason (in other words, was motivated) to come to the meeting or whether her 'motivation' was constructed through the conversational process is impossible to tell. Either way, the therapist's assumption of motivation was a necessary ingredient in his questions.

From this position, various assumptions about the therapeutic relationship suggest themselves:

1. The 'problem' is something that the client wishes to change. When clients talk about their problems, the worker will seek to acknowledge that these are indeed areas of difficulty for the client and to validate their feelings. If, however, the worker assumes that there may be underlying meanings to problems, it becomes increasingly difficult to keep central the client's narrative, as the worker's expert knowing becomes increasingly dominant.

2. The worker with a solution focused approach will have no goal other than that formulated by the client. In a statutory context, the worker will seek to establish what the client can hope to achieve within the requirements of the statutory authorities and the law.

3. Just as the worker will work towards the client's goal, the worker will also trust the client to know when the work is done and whether or not it has been useful. Clients already bring to the work of therapy the resources, skills, and strengths that they need to resolve the problem. It may be that the client does not know this yet and the worker therefore will be asking herself how she might talk with the client so that the client notices.

4. The worker should attempt to have no view about what the client should/could do to resolve the problem that they bring. It is the job of the worker and the client together, through

their talking, to formulate what will be this client's unique way of resolving this situation at this time, while allowing space to clarify what is right for the client in the specific context of their values, beliefs, and culture.

5. Whatever the client does we assume to be their best way of being helpful to the therapeutic process. When the worker reads the client's response as indicative of 'resistance', this is a cue for the worker that they are not listening hard enough to the client and probably need to do something different. There are no 'wrong' answers in SFBT whatever the client's answer may be.

6. The expertise of the therapist lies in having access to ways of talking with and thinking about clients that are associated with the client finding ways of resolving the problem that has brought them to therapy. The therapist's job is to build questions from the client's answers, most often incorporating their last words into a new question, which will lead the client to further self-discovery. In this sense, the client's relationship with himself is more important than his relationship with the therapist.

The evidence that Solution Focused Brief Therapy works

For a relatively youthful approach, the evidence that SFBT works has been accumulating very rapidly. At the time of writing, Macdonald (2011) points to 97 relevant studies, two meta-analyses, 17 randomized controlled trials showing benefit from the solution focused approach, and 9 showing benefit over and beyond existing methods. Of the 34 comparison studies, Macdonald states that 26 favoured a solution focus. Macdonald also highlights effectiveness data for over 4000 cases that suggest a success rate of more than 60 per cent within 3–5 sessions. The studies that he cites range across therapy and counselling, including the field of offending and substance misuse (Lindforss and Magnusson 1997), domestic violence (Lee *et al.* 1997), group work with couples and parents (Zimmerman *et al.* 1996, 1997), work with older people (Seidel and Hedley 2008), physical difficulties (Cockburn *et al.* 1997), mental health (Eakes *et al.* 1997; Perkins 2006), as well as work with children (Lee 1997) and in education (Littrell *et al.* 1995; Franklin *et al.* 2008). The potential range of applications for the approach evidenced by these studies is impressive and indeed so far none of the studies point to clear and evident exclusion criteria. Demographic differences do not make sufficient difference to allow potential clients to be excluded on demographic grounds, the nature of the problem does not seem to be significant, and not all studies have even shown a difference on the basis of chronicity, although Macdonald's studies (Macdonald 1997, 2005) do show a difference in the expected direction.

Thus at present the state of knowledge regarding the approach suggests effectiveness across a wide range of presentations and good comparability with other treatments. This would potentially allow ethical practitioners to attempt SFBT in all referrals. However, Beyebach's work in Salamanca (Herrero de Vega 2006) is also helpful and supports the core solution focused rule, 'if it doesn't work, do something different', since his research suggests that if after three sessions there is no improvement a change of model or a change of therapist is indicated.

As regards the long-lastingness of change, the most helpful study is that by Isebaert (de Shazer and Isebaert 2003) on his work in the field of alcohol use from the St. Jean Hospital in Bruges, Belgium. Isebaert's work, which includes a mixture of out-patient, day-patient, and in-patient interventions based on SFBT as the core model of intervention, shows approximately 50 per cent of the sample abstinent at 4 years and a further 25 per cent controlled drinking. These are quite outstanding figures and serve to challenge the idea that any brief therapy is by its nature productive in the short term only.

13

How brief is 'brief'?

Solution focused work has been delivered over the years in many contexts and has been variously packaged. In schools and doctors' surgeries as well as through Employee Assistance Programmes, SFBT has been offered on a fixed-term basis, over four or six or in exceptional circumstances eight sessions. Solution focused groupwork has similarly been offered on a time-limited basis, and others have experimented with single-session – albeit lengthy session – work. However, traditionally SFBT has been regarded as a *brief* rather than as a *time-limited* or *short-term* therapy. And the definition of 'brief' developed early on by Steve de Shazer remains the definition that practitioners most often cite: 'as long as it takes and not one session more' (statement made during presentation organized by BRIEF in 1990). So solution focused brief work is founded on a client-determined brevity. It will be the client who decides how brief *brief* in fact turns out to be, since it will be the client who will determine at what point enough has been achieved. Interestingly, despite giving the client the power to decide whether or not to return for more sessions, the typical solution focused brief therapy is shorter than many of the so-called short-term, time-limited packages, with Macdonald pointing in his summary of the research findings to average interventions of between three and five sessions. At BRIEF, clients have for many years attended, on average, fewer than four times and recently there has been evidence that this figure has been declining.

To explain this apparent paradox – an open-ended offer ending in markedly time-limited interventions – we highlight a number of key assumptions in solution focused work:

1. There is no need for an initial assessment stage and work with the client can start at once.
2. The task is not to initiate a process of change but to highlight the fact that change is already happening – much of the work

of therapy will already have been completed prior to the first meeting, just that the client may not have noticed.

3. Clients bring with them solution patterns as well as problem patterns and change is based on doing more of things that the client is already doing.

4. Whatever the client is doing is the best that the client can do in the present, and therefore it is the job of the therapist to collaborate with the client's best ways of working. This thought enables the therapist to avoid time-consuming (and expensive) battles with the client's supposed resistance.

5. Interventions are based on the client's own best hopes for the work and therefore stay close to the client's motivation and thinking.

6. Each session is treated as if it may be the last.

7. The solution focused approach, emerging from the systemic world, believes that 'a change in one element of a system or in one of the relationships between elements will affect the other elements and relationships which together comprise the system' (de Shazer 1985: 43) and that, in the nature of a ripple effect, 'only a small change is necessary to initiate change in a system' (1985: 17).

8. Solution focused work tends to longer between-session intervals, giving the client the time to do something different. Thus a four-session piece of work may take place over 10 weeks or more.

9. Solution focused practitioners tend to believe that most clients have better ways to spend their time than talking to therapists and therefore will think of therapy as a short intervention in people's lives that enables people in distress to reconnect with their resources in such a way that they are enabled to again get on with their lives.

Solution focused brief therapists therefore bring to their work a set of assumptions that maximize the likelihood that the work will be time-efficient.

Summary: the structure of solution focused sessions

A first solution focused session is likely to follow the pattern of establishing the hoped-for outcome, eliciting a description of what this outcome might look like and finding out what foundation might already be in place on which to build. These three areas of focus are reflected in three key questions from which all others are developed:

1. What are your best hopes from our meeting(s)?
2. What will be different in your life if these hopes are achieved?
3. What is already in place that will contribute to these hopes becoming a reality?

A solution focused brief therapist will not need to stray beyond this framework if she or he is to provide successful therapy briefly.

Different therapists will have their own preferred order when it comes to the second and third questions but all will begin with the first because without knowing the desired endpoint, it is not possible to steer the conversation in the right direction. Once the hoped-for outcome has been agreed, one therapist might choose to establish the foundation, what is already happening that might provide a firm platform from which to set off into a better future. Another therapist might choose to have the client describe his or her preferred future first and then look back from this vantage point to its history. Occasionally in a first session it turns out that the client has already made considerable progress. One desperate mother brought her child only to report that he had already made improvements. The therapist began by asking the boy what his mother meant. Thirty minutes later the therapist had a list of forty improvements that the boy and his mother had noticed. It was the last session and all the clients' own work.

In the next section, we begin the process of describing the nuts and bolts of solution focused practice. We will base this upon our current ideas and practice at BRIEF, and use case examples from our own work. We present a simple summary below of the main elements of our solution focused practice. It is important to bear in mind that these are not 'rules' to which the therapist has to adhere; they are only guidelines.

The first session

1. *Opening*. Many therapists will want to begin their work, as in other approaches, by getting to know the client. In solution focused practice, we call this stage 'problem-free talk', to indicate an interest in the person, not the problem. We regard this stage as optional.

2. *Contracting*. SFBT is a client-centred approach, and it is therefore essential that the therapist discovers from the outset what the client wants to achieve from meeting with them. 'What are your best hopes from the work?' is the question developed by BRIEF (George *et al.* 1999: 13).

3. *Describing the preferred future*. Having established the client's hopes from the work, the next stage is to invite the client to describe how he would know, in everyday terms, that his best hopes were achieved. The 'Tomorrow Question', as we call it, 'suppose you achieved your hopes overnight, what would you be doing tomorrow?' is the question most used at BRIEF.

4. *Identifying instances of success that are already occurring*. Once the client's preferred future has been described in detail, the therapist will search for signs of that future already happening in the client's life, whether currently or in the recent past; anything they are doing or have done that fits with the achievement of their preferred future. *Scaling questions* are frequently used to enable clients to rate their progress, with 10 representing their preferred future achieved; assuming they are above 0 (or have been before), this gives them the chance to describe what they are already doing that is working, as well as to ascertain what might be small signs of progress in future.

5. *Closing*. Shortly before the end of the meeting, the therapist might take a short break to reflect on what the client has said that is useful. The therapist will then summarize the session, acknowledging what the client has been struggling with and giving appreciation for the hopes they have expressed and any successes they may already have had. The aim is to highlight whatever the client has said that could be associated with the client making further progress.

Follow-up sessions

In the second and subsequent sessions, we are following up on the client's progress towards their preferred future and therefore the opening question is usually 'What's better since we last met?'

It is as if the therapist is starting at stage 4 in the schema above. There is usually no requirement to explore 'best hopes' or the 'preferred future' again. The therapist will often revisit the scale to ascertain progress the client has made, and to find ways to amplify and consolidate it. Where clients report no progress or that things are worse, the therapist has many options, including the use of coping questions and looking for exceptions to the problem.

Part 2

FEATURES OF
SOLUTION FOCUSED
INTERVIEWING

15

Ideas about therapeutic conversation

Therapy is a form of conversation but a conversation directed towards a purpose rather than one to be enjoyed for itself. In SFBT, the client always defines the purpose of therapy. The conversation is then directed towards that end. Though a full understanding of the conversational process might be beyond us, there are two simple ideas that help define it:

1. Turn-taking.
2. Each turn following and building on the previous turn.

The turn-taking idea allows everyone to have a say and so participate in shaping and defining the world we live in. It is a rule most often noticed when it is broken, for example, by interruption. If others take our turn too often, or if for any other reason we do not have a voice, we become marginalized and diminished. This is the experience of many of our clients and all disenfranchised individuals and groups. The equality of opportunity for each person to have a voice is possibly the most important equality and, in the therapy room at least, this can be afforded each client provided the therapist is disciplined enough to speak in turn.

The second idea, that each turn builds on what has gone before is necessary for creativity and for therapy to be effective. Each conversation if these two ideas are followed will help 'co-create' a constantly evolving view of the world. The therapist's task is to influence this view in the client's favour by careful choice of questions.

16

Choosing the next question

In everyday conversations, we do not usually pay conscious attention to how we choose each of our contributions; if we did, we might well sound false and stilted. Professional conversations are different and what we ask should be governed by what questions we think might be useful to the client or essential to the task in hand. As we listen to what a client is saying, we need to formulate our next question so that it builds on what the client is saying in what we hope will be a creative and useful way. When the client's answer is multifaceted, the choice of response is not always easy. Take the following response to the question, 'what are your best hopes from this therapy?':

> I'm not really sure. I've suffered from depression most of my adult life just as my mother did. There are days when I give up and just stay all day in bed. My husband says he's fed up and most evenings he's down the pub. I suppose I just want to feel better.

It is certainly not possible to follow up on every aspect of this response, so a choice has to be made. The therapist's model or theory will largely determine how the choice is made. Models with theories of causation will look for causes: historical theories might pick up on the mother's depression; a systemic model might be interested in the marital relationship and look for a link between that and depression; a cognitive therapy might be interested first in exploring the thoughts about 'giving up'. A solution focused brief therapist would be listening for that part of the client's response that answered the question, 'what are your hopes *from* this therapy'. The description of such difficulties would affect the tone in which the next question was asked but the question would most certainly follow the hope 'to feel better', for instance, 'What might be the first sign to you that you were beginning to feel better?'

It has been said that the most commonly asked question in SFBT is 'what else?' Trainees sometimes joke that 'when in doubt, ask "what else"!' It is true that this question is the simplest method for inviting the client to add to their description. For example, if the client in the above example answered with 'I'd be getting out more often', and the therapist then asked 'what else?', the client might answer 'I'd call a friend I haven't spoken to in ages'. On the other hand, the therapist could have asked 'where might you go to?' and have focused the conversation for the next few minutes on where she went to, who she met, what difference it made to her, and so on, and *then* asked 'what else would tell you were beginning to get better?' The difference between these questions can be characterized (based on Tohn and Oshlag 1997) as *broadening* and *detailing*[1]. Both are used in solution focused interviewing (see Chapter 41).

The whole of this book could be seen as a system for choosing the next question.

---

[1] Thanks to Guy Shennan for his rephrasing of Tohn and Oshlag's original description.

17

Acknowledgement and possibility

The importance of being where the client is cannot be overstressed, especially with a model that looks to the future. Being solution focused does not mean being problem-phobic. It is as important to acknowledge where the client is as it is to explore the possibilities of where he or she might be (O'Hanlon and Beadle 1996). As in any therapeutic approach, the therapist needs to listen carefully and with interest to everything the client chooses to say. How the therapist then responds depends a great deal on the particular approach. Having listened carefully to the client's answer, the therapist will choose which of its elements will form a platform for the next question. A model based on tracing historical causes might follow a client's account of a problem with: 'That must have been very difficult, when did it begin?' A strengths-based therapist might say: 'That must have been very difficult, how did you manage to handle it?' In both examples the client is likely to feel acknowledged but in the latter there are more obvious seeds of possibility. Paradoxically, within the solution focused model, the greater the hardship, the more multiple and intractable the problems appear, the greater is the achievement of managing to live with them. Recognizing survival strengths such as perseverance and determination opens the way to future possibility: 'If all this struggle pays off and you eventually turn a corner, what do you think the first sign might be?'

The following example is of a 5-year-old boy, Abel, on the verge of permanent exclusion from school. His mother was seriously disabled by multiple sclerosis and on bad days had just begun needing a wheelchair. Her prognosis was poor. The work began alone with the class teacher Miss Brown, Abel's mother having declined to attend. Miss Brown was obviously distressed, partly by Abel's extreme behaviour and possibly even more by the challenge he presented to her view of her competence. After a long description, the therapist commented on Miss Brown's perseverance and asked how she still managed to teach her class when Abel demanded so much of her attention. She said it was very difficult and it was because the class was suffering that exclusion was being considered. Though a referral for therapy was a necessary step in the exclusion process, the therapist chose to see it more constructively and asked what Miss Brown saw in Abel that gave her hope that therapy might work. She said that when Abel sang, he was like a little angel and she could see that behind the behaviour there was a very likeable boy.

Having acknowledged the teacher's difficulty, recognized her competence, and located a small thread of hope, the therapist asked Miss Brown how she would know that the therapy was having a positive effect. She said she would know from the moment he walked in and with a little prompting described him performing the morning ritual of almost every infant school in Britain: sit quietly on the mat, answer when your name is called for the register, stand quietly in line, and walk quietly to assembly.

Two days later, the therapist met with Abel and his mother, Gloria. She was even more distressed than Miss Brown, seeing her illness and impending death as the cause of Abel's troubles and especially upset that being excluded would lose her son the chance of an education and therefore blight his life. She was angry with the school and vowed to fight them over the exclusion. When asked, Gloria said she had always been a fighter, had needed to be. She was even fighting the wheelchair because she wanted to be a 'normal' mum for Abel. 'And if the fighting pays off, how will you know it was worth it?' To this question, inviting possibility in the wake of strength and determination, Gloria said: 'He'll come home from school happy'. As in any solution focused conversation, a description of Abel's happy behaviour gave substance to the possibility. Abel, too, wanted to be happy at school. He liked Miss Brown and also liked behaving well because she was nice to him. The therapist asked if he knew how to behave well. Abel nodded and with encouragement went on not only to describe but to enact 'good behaviour' at the beginning of the day. With his mum and the therapist he sat longest and quietest on the mat, was the least fidgety while lining up, and was able to lead the way round the therapy room without saying a word.

Interestingly, Abel's behaviour changed dramatically at school the day after the meeting with Miss Brown and before his meeting with the therapist. It seems Miss Brown was already on the verge of turning the corner.

18

Compliments

A feature of SFBT from the very start has been ending a session with affirmative feedback to the client. It is a disciplined and thoughtful process. A lazy or patronizing comment will do no harm to the client but it will certainly undermine the credibility of the therapist. Compliments, therefore, need to have certain characteristics. They need to be honest and evidence-based, so if the client asks the basis of a compliment the therapist can point to a specific behaviour described by the client. They need to be relevant to the client's purpose for being in therapy and they need to relate to something the client has achieved, preferably with effort. They also have to be given in a way that the client can accept and can agree with. Compliments cannot be used to persuade the client into accepting the therapist's view, as when we mistakenly think we ought to 'point out the positives'. A client may say he lacks confidence yet behave as if he has it. The therapist would not say, 'I think you have lots of confidence because of your behaviour here'. Instead, he might say, 'How have you found a way to act confidently even though you don't feel it?'

Finally, a compliment must have no strings attached; it should be unconditional and not be used to try to pressure the client into behaviour the therapist would like to see. A typical conditional compliment such as 'you have done really well with this homework, keep it up' is unlikely to be taken seriously, since it so clearly comes from the giver's agenda.

As a solution focused therapist becomes more practised, many compliments will be built into questions: 'How did you manage to turn in such good homework given all the difficulties you are facing at the moment?' is both affirmative and acknowledging. But the new solution focused practitioner will do well to stick with the ritual of ending each session with compliments because this will influence his or her attention *during* the session.

If compliments have to be given at the end, the therapist has no choice but to look for strengths and achievements during the session. This will help the session stay on the solution focused track.

19

Deciding who to meet with

As discussed in Chapter 13, SFBT first developed within the family therapy tradition in which systems theory plays a dominant role. A legacy of this early connection is the assumption that change in one part of a system – whether it be a family, a team, a friendship group or an organization – will lead to changes in other parts of the system. This ripple effect of change was borne out by de Shazer's early research, which showed that issues and relationships not discussed in therapy were still positively affected by the process (de Shazer 1985: 147–154). Research at BRIEF (Shennan and Iveson 2011) has supported this view, that who attends sessions has no obvious correlation with outcome. The same percentage of clients reported improvement (or lack of it) irrespective of who attended. Even attendance by the 'identified patient' does not seem to be necessary.

If who attends makes little or no difference to outcome the therapist has no knowledge on which to base a recommendation, so when a client is referred and wants to know who should attend, a solution focused therapist is likely to ask for the client's opinion, since the client is the person most knowledgeable about the circumstances. Typically, the therapist will say:

> To be honest, we don't know you well enough to make a recommendation, we just know that some people like to come alone, some like to come with the whole family, some would like to come but can't afford to take a day off work or school so we'll trust your judgement. Have a think about it and decide who you think should come and we'll start from there. We can always do something different later.

Clients appreciate the chance to make an informed decision and also that therapy can fit into life's needs like earning a living and getting an education. And at no point does the therapist hypothesize negative reasons for any person's absence; whoever attends are the right people to be there and whoever is absent has other things to be getting on with.

Part 3

GETTING STARTED

20

Problem-free talk

Problem-free talk is a simple practice with three purposes:

1. It enables the therapist, within the first few minutes of meeting a new client, to meet the 'person' rather than the 'problem'.
2. It allows the therapist to 'choose' the client with whom she is going to work.
3. It begins the process of 'resource-gathering', which will equip client and therapist with the necessary means to solve whatever problems have brought them together.

The practice involves spending a few minutes asking the client about any aspect of his life that does not involve the problems he is bringing to therapy. It might begin with 'Tell me about yourself', 'Have you come far?', 'What do you do?' ('How do you spend your day?' was a favourite of de Shazer) or any other expression of interest in the client's life. As the conversation proceeds, the client comes into view as a *person* rather than the 'collection of problems' that often make up a referral.

In the following example, Yasmin Ajmal, a former colleague at BRIEF, begins talking with her client Robert who has just turned 9 years old and was referred by his school.

Therapist:	What have you been doing at school today?
Robert:	[enthusiastically] Science.
Therapist:	Is that something you like?
Robert:	Yes.
Therapist:	Tell me what you've been doing in science.
Robert:	We've been learning about electricity.
Therapist:	And what have you learned?
Robert:	How it can electric shock you.
Therapist:	Oh.

Robert:	And about rubber round the wire so it doesn't electric shock you. And we've made our own circuits.
Therapist:	Tell me about that – are these circuits with wire?
Robert:	Yes with wire and lights and motors.
Therapist:	That sounds very interesting.
Robert:	I got a box and made wheels and lights, two lights and motors and made the box in the shape of a car.
Therapist:	Really!
Robert:	Yes and I put four motors in it.
Therapist:	Four motors! Why four? Was it to make it go faster?
Robert:	To give it more power.
Therapist:	I see.
Robert:	And I turned it on and the lights came on and it drove forward.
Therapist:	Really! And did it go fast?
Robert:	Yes. I couldn't catch it!
Therapist:	Why, because it was going so fast?
Robert:	Yes. It fell off the table into a pot of water and broke.
Therapist:	Oh dear!
Robert:	But I didn't mind.
Therapist:	You didn't mind, because?
Robert:	Because I knew how to make it again.

This sequence lasts for less than three minutes and the Robert who comes into focus is an enthusiastic, confident, generous, and socially skilled boy. He is polite, cooperative, humorous, articulate, and extremely likeable, the sort of boy any teacher would be happy to join the class and any parent would be pleased to see their own children playing with. It is this Robert that Yasmin 'chooses' to work with rather than the Robert described in the referral letter, who was a boy close to permanent exclusion from school. In subsequent work, which extends over four sessions, Yasmin keeps the competent, collaborative Robert by her side and together they find his own unique pathway to a more rewarding and successful life at school.

Like much in the solution focused repertoire, 'problem-free talk' is adapted from ordinary conversational practice that we have all learned from birth. If when we met new people socially for the first time we began to enquire about their problems, social life on Earth would have been cut off at birth. Socially, we begin conversations by looking for common ground and looking for what we might like and value in the other person. Solution focused therapists have adapted this common practice as a therapeutic tool.

21

Identifying resources

BRIEF's first course was organized as a series of two-hour evening sessions. In the first session, the themes were problem-free talk and identifying (and naming) resources. The feedback at the second session a week later was quite extraordinary. Many participants reported significant changes in their clients, including in two cases an apparent resolution of the presenting problem. The only difference to their own behaviour had been to begin with problem-free talk and alongside whatever else they did they looked for the client's resources.

What emerged from analysing these changes was that, because the therapist was spending at least some of the time focusing on the resourceful side of their clients, the clients were becoming more open. This was leading to a different quality in the conversations, which in turn led to more rapid change than had been expected.

Although 'strength-based' approaches are now more common, many professionals still remain shy of identifying their clients' resources, claiming the practice is over-optimistic, as if seeing a client's strengths will somehow prevent a clear sight of their problems. This would be like an accountant not noting a company's assets in case it caused blindness to its debts. For this an accountant would be struck off. With every therapeutic approach that works, it works, in the end, because the client has been helped to draw in some different way on their resources: therapy doesn't change people, it enables them to discover their own resources so they can make the changes themselves. Discovering and attending to the client's resources is an essential element of solution focused practice.

Leidl had been coming for therapy for over two years. Even though it was only at monthly intervals, the meetings had become repetitive and with no clear end in sight. The therapist was becoming despondent (and no doubt Leidl was, too) and then he found himself beginning to dread Leidl's next visit. One of solution focused practice's self-supervisory procedures for situations such as these, when the therapist begins to lose hope for the client, is to do a 'resource audit'. Fifteen minutes before the next session, the therapist sat down and wrote a list of Leidl's many achievements in life, not least, by her own wits, surviving the Holocaust. He noted her resourcefulness, determination, perseverance, sense of humour, resilience, generosity, compassion, honesty, and capacity for hard work. Fifteen minutes later, the Leidl he had described entered the room for what turned out to be her penultimate session. Sometimes, if we don't take the time to identify and name a client's resources we begin to lose sight of them, and this can be very bad news for the client. Luckily for Leidl, the therapist redeemed himself in time and, very soon afterwards, she declared herself cured of the depression that had dogged her life since her wartime escape.

22

Listening with a constructive ear: what the client *can* do, not what they cannot do

To listen with a constructive ear requires an about turn from most therapeutic listening (Lipchik 1986) or at least those therapies based on psychological theories. These theories offer explanations of human behaviour: they tell us how humans operate in order for us to understand what is going on. What is sometimes forgotten is that these theories are only metaphors, usually taken from the physical world. They range from the Rolls Royce engine of Freudian psychoanalysis to the simple belt and braces of Pavlovian behaviourism, and as there are now more than 400 of them it is safe to say that none represent an objective truth. They are just ways of looking at human behaviour. These theories usually require us to investigate the facts to allow us to make an assessment of the problem and then decide on the appropriate treatment. To do this we need to listen for information about the problem and our questions will therefore follow this listening: 'When did it begin?', 'What sort of relationships did your parents have?', 'Have you always been attracted to this kind of person?' Though different psychological theories will lead to different questions, they are mostly of the 'get to the bottom of it' investigative variety intended to discover what is wrong. They are not constructive questions, ones that search out the building blocks of new possibilities.

Constructive listening does not mean that the client's problems go unacknowledged. SFBT is no different from any other therapy in that it seeks to start with where the client is and not where the therapist would like them to be. This does not mean that the client has to retell their whole story, nor that the therapist needs to seek information about the problem story. Instead, the problem is used to redefine achievement. As mentioned previously, the more serious the problem, the greater the client's achievement in coping with it. A question such as the following both addresses the problem (indirectly) and directs curiosity towards the client's strengths and resources: 'Given how down you've been feeling the last few days, and given how hard it is for you to use public transport, how did you find the wherewithal to keep your word and honour this appointment?'

Gladys had left psychiatric hospital very recently and was relating the trials and tribulations of her return home to a house with a burst water pipe, which required the attention of several workmen over the course of a day and evening. Gladys had been admitted after an overdose and had begun her story by wondering if she shouldn't ask to be taken back on the ward. She finished her story by saying she was so upset by 2 am when the work was finished that she forgot to thank the workmen so ran out after them calling, 'Thank you very much, boys. They don't make them like you anymore!' Gladys then smiled and said, 'Heaven knows what the neighbours thought!'

The therapist asked her how she kept her sense of humour after such a distressing and even, for her health, dangerous time. 'You have to laugh, don't you?' was Gladys's response. The therapist suggested that not everybody is able to draw on a sense of humour at such difficult moments. In the ensuing conversation, Gladys recounted how friendly the workmen had been, how they had had a chat and a laugh together, and how if she had been 40 years younger she might have been tempted. By the end of the session Gladys was feeling justifiably proud of the way she had weathered what could have been a serious crisis. She also realized that she had woken up the next day feeling more positive about life than she had for some time, saying as she left: 'That hospital must have done a better job than I thought'.

Constructive histories

Constructive listening, by which the solution focused brief therapist uses to build the next question, directs us to the 'story behind the story'. For each account of hardship there is a story of struggle, for each setback a story of perseverance, and for each misfortune a story of survival. The solution focused therapist will listen carefully to the spoken story and then direct his or her therapeutic curiosity towards the not-yet spoken story.

Gerard was referred with chronic depression. He was 70, ram-rod straight, and had been depressed since he was 'blown up as a young man on active service'. This was the beginning of a 45-year story that took the best part of an hour to relate. During the story the therapist asked only eight questions, each one intended to create a more constructive view of events. The questions illustrate the use of a 'constructive ear':

1. How have you managed to keep going while suffering depression for so long?
2. How did you manage to cope with divorce on top of your depression?
3. What did your employer see in you that led them to give you such a responsible job?
4. How on earth did you overcome your alcoholism when you were in such dire straits?
5. How did you overcome your drug addiction?
6. Where did you find the confidence to speak to her let alone ask her out?
7. How did she know that behind the sad façade was a man worth marrying?

By this point Gerard was distinctly more upbeat and for the first time began to talk of the good luck in his life and how he was giving something back by driving a children's train at his local park. The therapist's final question was:

8. Gerard, answer me this: how, after suffering 45 years of depression, going through a painful divorce, losing your job as a trainee train driver, becoming an alcoholic and then a drug addict, did you not only fall in love but end up fulfilling your childhood ambition to be a train driver?

Gerard's response was, 'I told you it was an unusual life story'. The therapist could only agree. Three weeks later the referring community psychiatric nurse rang to say that Gerard had asked to come off his medication and was showing no signs of withdrawal.

24

Pre-meeting change

Pre-meeting change is one of the great 'secrets' of brief therapy. In the solution focused field it was identified in 1987 (Weiner-Davis *et al.* 1987) but Freud had also recognized the phenomenon. Within Freud's theory such early change was seen as a pathological failure to face up to problems and he dubbed it 'flight into health' (Freud 1912). In solution focus, it is seen as the same form of spontaneous recovery we have all experienced when we have found ourselves at the doctor's free of the symptoms that led us there.

Anyone with a troubleshooting role will know of this phenomenon: a problem is presented, a time fixed to deal with it, and between the two a resolution is somehow found. The obvious answer is not that the client has taken flight into health but rather, on committing himself to the possibility of a solution, finds himself, perhaps unconsciously, open to new and different thoughts about the problem and is thus more likely to find a solution. Weiner-Davis's research found that 70 per cent of clients experience some positive pre-meeting change and that the identification of this change was associated with a good prognosis. To capitalize on this natural process, many solution focused therapists ask new clients when making a first appointment to 'look out for any changes between now and when you come'.

George had been referred by his GP because of his anxiety and depression. He was one of two partners in a thriving business. The initial friendship between the two had deteriorated and George felt that he was being bullied. He blamed himself for not standing up to his partner, thought himself weak and unworthy, and was contemplating leaving the business. His marriage was close to breakdown and he could see no future. His hope from the therapy was to regain his self-respect and confidence and then stand up to his partner. In the early part of the session, George described the difference confidence and self-respect would make to his life at work and how this would give him the strength to stand up to his partner. When pressed for more detail, George said: 'like yesterday but without all the pathetic fear and worry that drags me down'. He then went on to describe how frightening he found being assertive, pointing to this as even more evidence of his weakness. The therapist then asked George to describe exactly what had taken place yesterday. His partner had brought an armful of files into the main office and in front of all the staff had berated George for his sloppy work, dropped the files at his feet, and told him to do his job properly. This had been the most blatantly bullying incident to date and 'something snapped' in George. Rather than pick up the files and take them meekly back to his office he called to his partner 'in an icy tone': 'If you would like me to look at the files again bring them to my office'. Leaving the files on the floor he turned and went to his own office. A few minutes later his partner, without a word, brought the files in.

Since then George had been in an agony of self-recrimination, berating himself for challenging his partner in public, replaying every moment with a critical eye, thinking of all the things he might have done differently, and totally failing to notice that he had stood up to his partner. He was now fearful that things would get worse but when asked how his partner had been that morning, he suddenly realized that he had been very friendly and suggested they go for a drink sometime like in the old days.

Not all pre-session changes are as dramatic as George's but most go unnoticed unless the therapist keeps a lookout. Once it is noticed, the client can immediately be recognized as someone who solves their own problems and the therapist is then able to take even more of the 'back seat' that characterizes solution focused brief therapy.

Part 4

ESTABLISHING A CONTRACT

25

Finding out the client's best hopes from the work

Within the first five minutes of most first meetings with a new client the solution focused practitioner will ask the client, 'So what are your best hopes from our talking together?' (George *et al.* 1999: 13). This simple question immediately highlights a number of the central characteristics of SFBT.

First, the question invites the client into a consideration of *outcome*, rather than an elaboration of the problem that has brought him to the meeting. If we ask the client 'what brings you here?', he is more than likely to respond with a description of the problem. Such questions generally have the effect of directing the client back towards his failed past and problematic present, inviting the client into problem-talk. Asking about the client's 'best hopes', however, invites the client into a picturing of a future state towards which he aspires to make progress. Indeed, the solution focused approach can be thought of as a *towards* approach, rather than an *away from* approach. Solution focused practitioners might perhaps compare themselves with taxi drivers. For example, if a new fare jumps into the back of the cab and when the driver asks 'where to mate?' the fare says 'away from the airport', the journey could turn out to be time-consuming and expensive. The taxi-driver wants to hear 'City please' and on following up with 'where exactly in the City' will be delighted to hear 'Newbury Street, round the corner from Barbican'. So the 'best hopes' question gently asks the client to specify his criteria for a successful therapeutic journey: 'What will it take for you to be able to say that coming here has been useful to you?'

In addition, this question has the effect of centralizing the client's perspective. The contract in SFBT is not based on the practitioner's perception of what may be required or on a process of assessment, but on the client's response to the 'best hopes' question. Therapists have traditionally made a distinction between the concepts of *want* and *need*. The client states what she *wants* but the therapist determines what that client *needs* based on a process of assessment leading to formulation. This distinction tends to construct a hierarchy of knowledge, characteristically assuming that what the client wants is in some ways superficial while the therapist's formulation, based on expertise and 'objectivity' (as if that were possible), has greater validity. Inevitably, this way of thinking can tend towards the trivialization of the client's knowledge. Solution focused therapists make no distinction between want and need. The solution focused practitioner chooses not to know better. What the client wants is, with a few exceptions that we will explore, the only legitimate foundation for the work and questions which the therapist asks that are not connected to the 'best hopes' answer are viewed as either impositional or impertinent, or indeed both.

The 'best hopes' question challenges clients. Many have come prepared to talk about the problem that is bothering them but state openly that they have given less thought to their preferred outcome. Some assume that therapy *is* talking about problems, and others who have previous experience of therapeutic interventions state that they have never been asked what they want. Focusing right from the beginning on the client's success criteria introduces a context of purposefulness and possibility to the work. It introduces a clear sense of direction. Without a defined outcome brevity is unlikely, since after all the client and therapist may not notice that they have arrived!

26

The 'contract': a joint project

So can it really be that simple? The practitioner asks the 'best hopes' question and whatever the client answers represents the contract for therapy. For the most part it is that simple and sometimes it is not. Harry Korman, a solution focused therapist in Malmo, Sweden, spelled out three criteria for the therapist to bear in mind during the negotiation of the 'contract' (Korman 2004):

1. something that the client wishes to achieve, which
2. fits with the practitioner's legitimate remit, and which
3. the practitioner and client working well together could hope to achieve.

The starting point, therefore, is indeed simple.

Therapist:	So what are your best hopes from our talking together?
Client:	I'm not sure really – I've been feeling pretty down recently.
Therapist:	Hmm. So what are your best hopes from coming here?
Client:	Just to feel better – better in myself.
Therapist:	Okay. So if you were feeling better in yourself, what difference are you hoping that would make?
Client:	Well I suppose I'd have that bit more confidence, I'd be liking myself more and I'd be getting on with life again rather than hiding away.

| *Therapist*: | So if at some point following our talking you found yourself more confident, liking yourself more and getting on with life again, that would tell you that this had been of use to you? |
| *Client*: | Yes, definitely. |

Here the process is straightforward. In answer to the therapist's question, the client specifies three life differences that will fit with most therapists' legitimate remit and which could, in most circumstances, be judged perfectly possible to achieve. Later in this section, we will examine what options the therapist might have when faced with more challenging responses to contract-seeking questions.

27

The difference between outcome and process

The solution focused approach is both client centred and outcome focused and yet, as we have seen, this does not mean that the solution focused practitioner will accept the first answer that the client gives to the question, 'So what are your best hopes from our talking together?' Not only does the contract have to fit with the worker's legitimate remit, and not only does the outcome have to be possible – in other words, within the client's realm of influence – but in addition the solution focused practitioner is looking for a response that represents an outcome rather than a process.

Imagine for a moment that when asked the best hopes question the client responds by saying, 'My best hope from our talking is just to get it all off my chest' or 'My best hope from all of this is just to understand, to understand why all this has happened'. While both answers fit with the criteria for a joint contract, neither represents an 'in-life' difference; indeed, both answers relate to the therapeutic process rather than to the everyday life of day-to-day experience. The solution focused practitioner assumes that clients are not merely curious about how their lives have developed, do not just wish to offload for the sake of it, but that they harbour these wishes for good reasons, and their reasons are life-related. The client imagines that 'understanding' or 'getting things off my chest' will make an 'in-life' difference, that it will lead the client somewhere that they want to go, and it is this that interests the solution focused practitioner, the desired destination, rather than a description of the assumed route.

The key question that will lead to the disentangling of route and destination, process and outcome, is simply 'so what difference will that make?' For example:

Therapist: If you were to get things off your chest, what difference are you hoping that that would make to you?

Client:	Well I'd just feel lighter, I'd feel better.
Therapist:	And if you were feeling lighter and feeling better, what are you hoping that that would lead to?
Client:	Just to have more energy, more positivity.
Therapist:	And if you were feeling that energy, that positivity, what might you notice yourself doing that you are not doing at present?

By the time the client responds to this question, her outcome will be firmly rooted in an 'in-life' difference.

Interestingly, this same route–destination distinction is also the basis for the solution focused practitioner's untangling of another set of client responses, where the response is so specific that the chances of the client being successful in the therapeutic process is restricted and the way forward is so tightly specified that there is little space for manoeuvre.

Therapist:	So what are your best hopes from our talking together?
Client:	Well I just have to have a job – I have been out of work so long that it is beginning to have a real impact on my life.
Therapist:	Okay – could I ask you some questions about that?
Client:	Sure.
Therapist:	If you had a job, what difference are you imagining that that would make to your life?
Client:	Well I'd feel better about myself – I'd feel like a useful member of society again.
Therapist:	And if you were feeling better about yourself, and feeling like a useful member of society again, what difference are you hoping that that would make?
Client:	Well, perhaps some of my confidence would come back and I'd be getting out and seeing people.

As soon as the outcome is defined in terms of confidence coming back, getting out, and seeing people, there are many ways that this can be achieved, maybe through getting a job, maybe even without. The client's chances of success have been enhanced through the disentangling of route and destination.

One final point. Throughout this book, we will use the phrase 'what are your best hopes *from* this . . . (work, meeting, etc.)' instead of 'what are your best hopes *for* . . .'. This small shift again points to the difference we have been discussing here, as 'best hopes for' will lead to the client thinking about what they want to work on in the session, which will be the process towards an outcome rather than the outcome itself. The latter is more likely to be achieved (but not guaranteed – hence the examples above!) by asking 'best hopes *from*'.

28

The 'Great Instead'

In most cases, people come to therapy bothered by problems. They feel depressed, they are arguing with their partners, they are shouting at their children, they are drinking too much, using drugs in an uncontrolled way, feeling anxious, feeling bad about themselves. And so when the therapist asks 'what are your best hopes?', very naturally the client's response stays close to those heart-felt concerns: 'I want to stop feeling so depressed', 'I won't be arguing with my partner', 'I won't be having all these negative thoughts'. If the solution focused practitioner were to accept any one of these propositions as the contract for therapy, the work is likely to be more 'problem focused' in the sense that a greater part of the talking is likely to focus on depression, on drug use, on anxiety or on alcohol, since it is not possible for people to talk about 'not being depressed', for example, without thinking about 'being depressed'. The negatively framed contract risks keeping the client focused on the problem that they want to leave behind, risks keeping alive, somewhat paradoxically, their sense of self as anxious, depressed, bad parent, failed partner. This continual focusing on the problem is likely to slow down the change process.

The bridge from a negatively framed focus to a positively framed focus is simply negotiated and the key word is 'instead'.

Therapist:	So *instead* of feeling depressed what would you like to feel?
Client:	I'd like to feel that I was getting on with my life again, I wasn't isolating, I wasn't hiding away.
Therapist:	Okay, so if you were getting on with your life again, what would you be doing *instead* of isolating, *instead* of hiding away?
Client:	I'd be getting out more, I'd be contacting people, and I'd be accepting invitations.

Within two or three questions, the client is moving away from 'not depressed' to beginning to describe the life that he would want to be living. So now therapy can focus on 'getting on with life', what that might mean to the client, and how the client can build a life that fits with that description rather than on 'reducing the impact of depression'. These two conversations, while closely connected – indeed, the client has indicated that one is the opposite of the other – are likely to have a markedly different effect. Talking about 'getting on with life' is likely to energize and enthuse, whereas talking about 'reducing depression' is likely to reduce the levels of energy and excitement in the conversation and keep the client connected to bothersome thoughts about 'why do I get depressed' or 'what has gone wrong with my life to make me so depressed'. This shift from solving the problem to building the solved state is central to becoming solution focused and is indeed definitional in highlighting the difference between a problem focused and a solution focused approach.

29

When the client's hope is beyond the therapist's remit

But what if the client responds to the therapist's enquiry with a hope that falls outside the therapist's realm of responsibility? For example, 'Look, in all honesty the only thing that would make a difference in my life would be being re-housed' (and the therapist has no role in relation to housing), or with a response that flies in the face of the therapist's responsibilities: 'All I want is never to have to come to this school ever again'. In both cases, the therapist's first job is to accept the client's answer: 'well that makes sense to me' or in the second case 'sounds like you've not been enjoying school much'. The second step is to clarify role: 'I guess you know that I have no influence with the housing department at all' or 'you do know that it is my job to make sure that you are in education don't you'. And then, step three, the negotiation to find a response that fits with what the worker can do.

Therapist:	Even though I can't influence the housing department, can I just ask this – if somehow you and your family were to be re-housed, what difference do you imagine that would make?
Client:	That's easy – we wouldn't be on top of each other all the time – we wouldn't be arguing so much – I wouldn't be so stressed – I'd be more patient with the children, I'd feel I was managing and there would be a light at the end of the tunnel.
Therapist:	Okay – suppose that even though you have not yet been re-housed and you don't even have any sort of time-scale for that from the department – yet nonetheless you realize that you are indeed beginning to see light at the end of the tunnel, and you are feeling that

	you are managing, would that make this useful?
Client:	Well yes I guess, although obviously what I really want is to be re-housed.
Therapist:	Of course and if we could move towards some light and some managing that would make this worthwhile?
Client:	Yes.

Here the worker has taken the client's wishes seriously, has been clear about his remit, and has moved to a 'hope' that is as close as possible to the client's original response.

30

When the client has been sent

The idea that 'being sent' conjures up is one of an involuntary client, someone who had no wish to attend and yet who somehow has ended up in the therapist's office 'against his will'. A moment's reflection begins to cast doubt on this. After all, even if seeing a therapist was not the client's own idea, somehow he has agreed to attend or at the very least has consented to walk into his room. On what basis has the client made this decision? The solution focused practitioner assumes that every client who agrees to talk has a good reason for doing this, and it is the task of the practitioner to discover what that reason might be. Sometimes the client's 'good reason' does not, at least initially, appear to coincide with the best hopes of the *referrer* from the work:

Therapist:	So what are your best hopes from our talking together?
Client:	I don't know really. My doctor wanted me to come.
Therapist:	So how come you decided to come?
Client:	Well, she thought that this could be good for me.
Therapist:	Great and if she turns out to be right, how will you know?
Client:	Well, I suppose that I would be managing my pain better.
Therapist:	Right, so if you were finding ways to manage your pain better I guess that that would be good for you – not just something that the doctor wants?
Client:	Of course it would.

In this example, within just a few questions the client is beginning the process of describing what she wants and all the practitioner had to do was to stay with the idea that the client chose to come even if it was not her idea.

Let's take a slightly tougher example where nonetheless the process is similar:

Therapist: So, what are your best hopes from coming here?

Client: Nothing really – my social worker said that I had to.

Therapist: And yet you came – how come you decided to do that?

Client: Well, they said at the conference that I had no chance of getting my children back unless I came to see you.

Therapist: Right – and that's something that you want to do – to get your children back?

Client: Of course!

Therapist: So to get the children back, is just turning up enough or do they want to see you making changes?

Client: No, there's a whole list of things. They want me to stop drinking, to talk about my abuse when I was small, to manage my anger better, to be more consistent with the kids, to be more reliable and something about self-esteem.

Therapist: Okay, so are they saying that if you do not make changes in these areas you won't get the children back?

Client: Yeah – even though I think I could have the kids back now and everything would be fine.

Therapist: Hmm. That's tough. Can I ask this – do you believe them? Do they mean what they say or are they just saying it?

Client: My solicitor says that they mean it and I have to come here if I want to have a chance in court.

Therapist: So even though you are not convinced that you need to make these changes, what do you think are the smallest signs that the social worker would need to see evidence of for you to have a chance of getting what you want, of getting the kids back?

Client: Well I suppose the drinking – seeing me arrive at the foster home on time, when I have said that I will, and not smelling of drink.

The practitioner will now build on this picture of required change and may well ask, 'So, are you prepared to have a go at this even though you are not sure it is needed, in order to get your children back?' If the client responds by saying 'yes', a response that is likely following this discussion, the work can proceed. What the practitioner must always remember is that what is important to the client is getting her children back from foster care and that the behavioural changes are only a means to that end.

31

Building a contract with young people

For those who work with children and young people, the experience of working with clients who are sent to a therapist is not unusual. Very few children have the idea independently that they would like to meet with a therapist. Indeed, almost all are sent by one of the adults in their lives – a parent, teacher, social worker or youth offending officer, for example.

A graceful way for the solution focused practitioner to recognize this is to start the session as follows:

Therapist: So, whose idea was it for you to come here to meet with me today?

Client: My mum – she wanted me to come.

Therapist: Right, so what are your mum's best hopes from our talking? How could she know that your coming here has turned out to be useful?

Client: She keeps going on about me changing my attitude. My teachers do too.

Therapist: Right – so is that just something that your mum and your teachers want or would that be good for you too?

Client: Well I suppose that it would be good for me too.

Therapist: Okay, so if something changed in relation to your attitude that would be useful to you too?

Client: Yes.

Therapist: So, is there anything else that would make this useful to you?

Client: Not really.

We can hear in this example the young person quite simply buying in to the adults' 'best hopes'. If, on the other hand, the young person had not bought-in, and had said 'not really, there's nothing wrong with me', the solution focused practitioner can then ask, 'Okay, you have come, you're not bothered by this attitude thing that other people are going on about, so what would stop this being a complete and utter waste of your time?' If then the young person responds by saying something along the lines of 'getting adults off my back', the therapist is in business again and the work has a direction.

32

When the client says 'don't know'

Steve de Shazer said that just as 'what else?' is the single most frequent question that the solution focused practitioner asks, so 'don't know' is the client's most frequent utterance. It is therefore important for the solution focused practitioner to have a way of thinking about this answer and a range of potential responses.

The simplest response on the practitioner's part is merely to wait. Many clients (especially young people!) seem to say 'I don't know' whenever asked a question, almost as a verbal tic, a habitual response, and if the practitioner waits long enough the client will begin to answer. For example, 'Well I suppose it would be my relationship with James, my youngest – he never does what I ask and I get furious – yes if things were better between us'. If after a short pause the client does not begin to respond, the practitioner can go back to the question, preferably changing it slightly, thereby acknowledging the client's 'don't know': 'So what do you think, what do you think might tell you that coming here had been useful to you?' The words 'think' and 'might' introduce a greater tentativeness to the original question, 'So, what are your best hopes from coming here?' The tentativeness allows for the client not to have to know and therefore makes it easier for the client to answer. If the client again answers 'I don't know', the practitioner can increase the tentativeness by saying, 'Have a guess – how do you imagine that you could know that our talking had ended up being of use to you?' If the client still answers 'I don't know', there remains a range of ways forward for the therapist.

Persistence

If the therapist chooses to persist, then giving some explanation as to why one is asking can be useful as can some 'normalizing' of the difficulty in responding. 'I know this is not an easy question – people have often given a lot of thought to what is bothering them but have not always thought so much about how they would know that therapy had been useful. But it really is important for me to have some idea of what you want from coming here, so that I have the best possible chance of getting this right for you. So what do you think . . .?'

Alternative perspective

Many solution focused practitioners have had the experience that clients often find it easier to answer from the perspective of another, rather than from their own. So the therapist can ask, 'So who knows you best?' 'My friend Jane' 'Okay, so how could Jane, without you saying a word to her about coming here, know that this has been useful to you?'

Referrer's perspective

An alternative starting point for clients who are finding it hard to specify their 'best hopes' is to track back through the 'best hopes' of the referrer. 'So whose idea was it for you to come here today?' 'My year head' 'Okay, so what are her best hopes from this?' If the client still finds it difficult to answer, then a meeting that includes the referrer and allows her to articulate her hopes as a basis for negotiation with the client can be useful.

The solution focused brief therapist assumes that every client who agrees to meet has a good reason for doing so (see example in Chapter 11). A key task of the therapist is to be sufficiently flexible in her approach to enable the client to articulate that good reason (George *et al.* 1999: 22–23).

33

When the client's hopes appear to be unrealistic

What if the client's first response is unlikely to happen as a result of the therapist and the client's talking together? One example is the child who responds to the worker's 'best hopes' question by saying that the only thing that would make a difference to her life is if 'mum and dad were back together again'. The therapist may know that both parents are happily settled in new relationships and that there is no likelihood of this happening even if it were to be the therapist's legitimate focus.

Therapist:	Yes of course – of course that would make a difference. I'm just not sure how that could happen as a result of the two of us talking together.
Client:	No I suppose not.
Therapist:	So, what would be your next best hope from our talking together?
Client:	Maybe if I had some friends – everyone else has friends.
Therapist:	Okay – can I ask you about that? . . . [pause] . . . If you did have friends, how would life be different for you?
Client:	I'd be happier, I'd feel more like the rest of my class, just normal.
Therapist:	So if we did some talking and you ended up feeling happier, feeling more like the rest of your class, maybe with more friends, that would make this useful to you?

In this example, the therapist accepts the child's wish for the parents to be together again, acknowledges that it is unlikely to happen as a result of their work together, and invites the child to specify a next best hope. Interestingly, the child comes up with another way to feel happier. If the child hadn't done, then the therapist would have had to go back to the hope, however unrealistic it was, and to ask how things would be for the child if the parents *did* get back together. It is quite possible that the conversation would then lead to the same endpoint, namely that the child would say he would be feeling happier and making friends, and the conversation can then look at ways of achieving those things even if the child's overall aim is not going to be achieved.

The above is one of many examples of situations where the therapist is led to raise the question of the *likelihood* of the outcome happening. Some therapists will ask the client to rate the likelihood of it happening on a scale where 10 = 'there's every chance it can' and 0 = 'no chance at all'.

'Best you can hope for'

Let's imagine sitting down with a client who in response to the 'best hopes' question says that she wants her boss to stop being so rude to her. The same question arises as occurs with the child cited above and yet we know that influence in relationships is complex and that change in any one part of a relational system can lead to change in another. The route that the therapist takes will depend on the client's answer to the question 'And how likely is that to happen?' If the client responds by saying 'I think she can change, there are whole days when she can be really nice', the solution focused practitioner will follow the client's lead and work on changing the boss, but if the client says 'no way, she's always been that way, she's that way with everyone, she seems to feel that she has to behave like an aggressive bloke', then another pathway is indicated. In this case, the therapist will respond to the client with 'Okay, so it doesn't look likely that she's ever going to change – so what's the best that you *can* hope for from coming here?' The framing 'the best that you *can* hope for' or 'your next best hope' are both useful responses in those situations where what the client really wants is not going to happen. Often, the client responds by saying, 'Well I guess that the best that I can hope for is just keeping my head down, getting through, so that I can get a good reference when I apply for another job'. This will prompt from the therapist,

'So, if you were keeping your head down in a way that was genuinely okay for you and was likely to get you the reference that you want, what difference would that be making to your day-to-day experience of work?'

Coping with life situations

Life's difficulties, the ones that most of us face, can generally be divided into 'problems', which are defined as potentially solvable, and 'life situations', those difficulties that cannot be solved. The distinction is simple and obvious. Although painful, bereavement, chronic illness, and loss are not *problems* because by definition they cannot be solved. There is an associated problem and it is remembering this that charts the way forward for both therapist and client, and that is the problem of *coping*, of *managing*, of *living with* the life situation. So if the client were to point to their chronic arthritic condition as their problem, the therapist is likely to respond by saying, 'Well I guess no amount of talking can take that away', and if the client agrees the therapist may well ask, 'So how will you know that you are managing your arthritis in the best possible way?'

34

What if there is a situation of risk?

The solution focused approach is a non-normative approach in the sense that it has within it no idea of right and wrong, no idea of how the client should live her life. The preferred outcome of the work is determined by the client, and the approach is merely a description of a way of talking with a client that is associated with the client achieving those preferred outcomes. Solution focus has no way of assessing or evaluating the client's life, it is in essence 'value-free' and the legitimacy of any question that the practitioner asks is determined by whether or not it can be related to the client's preferred outcome; if it cannot, then that question must certainly be regarded as impertinent, as intrusive but more than that it risks being impositional – the worker asserting his or her own sense of 'rightness' on the client.

This raises the question of how does the solution focused approach respond to risk and the short answer is that the solution focused approach does not! This does not mean however that the same practitioner, using the solution focused approach in her work, will not find a way of responding to risk, but to do so she will step outside the model and draw on an external set of values that can distinguish 'right' from 'wrong', safe from dangerous.

Imagine that a solution focused therapist is meeting with someone who states early on that that she has been violently beaten in the past by her partner and as a result of the assaults that she has suffered, her life has been put at risk. Further imagine that when asked her 'best hopes from the work', the client responds by saying that she wants to be more assertive, that she is fed up of being pushed around. From a solution focused point of view, this response presents no problems. The answer represents something that the client wants, that fits the worker's remit – helping people to be assertive – and the response represents a realistic possibility for the work. But for any worker alarm bells will be ringing. If the client asserts herself more, will her partner respond with increased violence to 'return her to her place'? And so the practitioner steps outside the model to draw the question of safety into the work.

Therapist:	All right, so you will know that this has been of use to you because you will be bringing more assertiveness to your life and in particular to your marriage?
Client:	Yes.
Therapist:	Okay – so can I ask you a question? I imagine that your safety is important to you too?
Client:	Of course it is.
Therapist:	Well then, let's imagine that your assertiveness is growing in a way that is good for you, good for your relationship and good for your safety – how will you know?

Here the client accepts the insertion of safety into the picturing of the preferred future, but it is important to recognize that the worker has 'imposed' the question of safety in an entirely legitimate way. If the client were to respond 'no' to the therapist's question, the therapist is left with a real ethical and moral dilemma. Does she carry on with the work or not? Solution focus cannot answer that question but an ethical practitioner has to.

35

When the practitioner is a gatekeeper to a resource

Many practitioners have complex and multiple roles, only one of which is the role of 'therapist'. Health professionals may be required to offer 'healthy living advice'. Drugs workers may be required to inform their clients of the risks of drug use. Social workers are routinely expected to monitor safety and risk in the lives of many of their clients. And many practitioners play an active role in decision-making regarding the allocation of resource. Although a social worker cannot necessarily independently decide on behalf of a department whether a young person is to be accommodated by the local authority, the desperate parent will realistically believe that gaining the social worker's support for accommodation represents a useful step towards the respite from stress and anxiety that they are seeking. And so when the solution focused social worker asks the parent about their 'best hopes', the parent may well respond by requesting, one way or another, that their child be removed. In such an instance, the social worker's task is similar to that of the educational psychologist faced with a school's wish for additional classroom support for a child deemed to have special needs, or a psychiatrist faced with a parent's request for medication for their child's 'hyperactivity'.

In each of these cases, the practitioner's task will include an assessment function and within that function each practitioner will be expected to conclude whether there could be a satisfactory 'resource-free' outcome; could the family resolve their difficulties with their child without accommodation, could the teacher find a way forward without the allocation of costly support, could there be a solution in relation to the child's behaviour that does not face the child with the label and the physical side-effects that come hand in hand with medication. A first step in the gauging of alternative possibilities is to find a way of opening a conversation that moves beyond the client's predetermined solution. Simply asking 'what difference are you hoping that that will make?' is likely to produce a response that opens up alternatives.

Client: Well, if you took him back into care I wouldn't have to be worrying every night what time he is going to come in and what he is up to, I wouldn't have the school on my back about his attendance, we wouldn't all be shouting and screaming at home, things would be quieter, we'd all be happier.

Therapist: Okay, sounds like things have been really tough again recently – and that's probably an understatement – and if I have understood things properly you want him to be coming in at a reasonable hour, you want him to be going to school, you want more quietness and happiness at home.

Client: Yes, you know what he's like – he takes no notice of me and at least things were better for the rest of us when he was at Stewart's Lodge.

Therapist: Right, so you also need him to take notice of you.

Client: Yes, of course.

Therapist: Right. Let me see if I've got this right – coming in at night, going to school, quietness and happiness at home, and Michael taking notice of you?

Client: Yes, but he's not going to – and I've had enough of it – it's no good for him, no good for Janine and William – I'm shouting and screaming all the time.

Therapist: Sure – and I'm sorry things have got like this – and you know that I cannot make a decision just like that without meeting Michael and probably meeting all of you together, so if we could find a way of him making those changes and of things being different at home, would that make it manageable?

Client: Yes, but it's not going to happen . . .
Therapist: And if it did would that makes things
              manageable?
Client: I suppose so.

No-one would assume that this piece of work with Michael and his mother and his family is going to be easy, and indeed he may end up being accommodated, but once the request is defined in terms of the wished for changes rather than merely accommodation, it becomes obvious that there are many potential routes towards that and that accommodation is just one of those routes.

36

What if we fail to develop a joint project?

If there is no joint project, the work is not solution focused. The work may be effective, it may be empowering, it may indeed be strengths-based, but it cannot be solution focused because every piece of work needs a direction and if the direction is not specified by the client it will inevitably, by default, be specified by the practitioner. And since the solution focused approach is non-normative, the therapist can have no way of knowing what the 'right' direction would be. How can the practitioner know what questions to ask, what to highlight, and what to let go by if she does not know the 'best hopes'? In such circumstances, the worker can make use of the whole range of solution focused questions and techniques, and doing so may well be useful, but using the techniques will not make the work solution focused if there is no defined joint project.

An obvious instance where there is (at least initially) no joint project is when the work is overtly – and indeed legitimately – worker-directed. Most statutory work at least in the opening stages takes this form. The practitioner's agency has concerns, often not shared by the client, and those concerns legitimate intervention in the client's life even in circumstances where the client does not agree with the concerns. In such circumstances, the practitioner will constantly be seeking 'buy-in' to the agency goals often through an open specification of the risks to the client if there is no change. For example, 'Look I know in the past you have never wanted to go back into hospital – is that still true?' If the client responds in the affirmative the practitioner can ask, 'So do you know what I would need to see different for you to have a better chance of staying out of hospital?' On the basis of a specification of the practitioner's minimum requirements, the client can be asked: 'So are you happy to work with me to make those changes so that you can stay at home?' Again if the client says 'yes', a joint 'staying-at-home project' has been established and the work can become solution focused but if not the practitioner will be working to his own goals.

During the course of the work there are likely to be many opportunities for the establishment of 'joint mini projects' and a key route to them is listening out for the client's complaints. Every complaint is a possibility: 'It sounds like that really bothers you, finding it hard to get out, would you like to see that changing?' If the client accepts this project, then within a larger piece of work, where the practitioner's goals are largely agency-determined, there will be a small solution focused project of 'getting out more'. In such circumstances, the work is 'twin-tracked' – a client track and the agency track. An invitation to twin-tracking can always be offered to clients at the beginning of a piece of work. 'I know that you disagree with us about our concerns about Daniel but as you know, I will be visiting regularly and it is my job to raise those concerns and I will do each and every time we meet. That's my job. Now while I am doing that what could you get out of our talking together that would make this at least a little worthwhile from your point of view?' If the client responds, then the work moves into twin-track, which holds more possibilities for the future of cooperation than single, agency-tracked work.

Part 5

THE CLIENT'S PREFERRED FUTURE

37

Preferred futures: the 'Tomorrow Question'

Once the therapist has an answer to the question, 'So, what are your best hopes from this therapy?' and has therefore discovered the client's purpose, the most usual next step is to begin to elicit a description of what the client's life would be like if these hopes were realized. In the early days of SFBT's development, this focus was seen as one in which the specification of goals allowed client and therapist to know when to stop meeting (de Shazer 1988). However, it was not long before the therapeutic value of this future focused conversation became apparent. It seemed that the more clearly a client could describe a hoped-for future, the more likely and quickly a positive outcome would follow. It was as if the description in words acted as a virtual experience for the client, thus creating a sense of possibility – that things really could be different. And the descriptions began to cover every aspect of the client's daily life, not just the issue that had brought him or her into therapy. Such wide-ranging coverage was not adequately represented by the notion of 'goals', which are more specific and circumscribed and the term 'preferred futures' was coined (Iveson 1994).

Strictly speaking, it is a mistake to see the client's description of a preferred future as a 'solution'. More accurately, it is an alternative way of living in which the presenting issues have no significant part. The solution to the client's problems develops as an outcome of successful therapy. For example, a mother might complain about a teenage daughter staying out late and her first response to the 'best hopes' question may be that her daughter comes home on time. The therapist will not want to make this the central focus of the work; instead, he will ask 'what difference might that make?', exploring this until he can establish a more 'quality of life' outcome such as 'we'd have a better relationship'. The task then would be to elicit a description of what this 'better relationship' would look like in the everyday life of the family. If the description does its work, the mother and daughter will begin to get on better and as a result of their improved relationship they are likely to be more able to negotiate rules. The 'problem' is solved by the family without any direct intervention by the therapist.

A trademark future focused question in SFBT has been the 'Miracle Question':

> Suppose that one night, while you were asleep, there was a miracle and this problem was solved. How would you know? What would be different? How will your husband know without your saying a word to him about it?

> (de Shazer 1988: 5)

Initially, before the 'best hopes' question was devised, the 'miracle' was a description of 'life without the problem'. Later, it became more logical to ask about 'life when the best hopes are achieved' (George *et al.* 1999: 28). The purpose of the 'miracle' metaphor was to overcome the client's sense of hopelessness, as miracles can do anything. Once the notion of hope was introduced to the very first question, 'miracles' proved less necessary and, as in the mother and daughter case above, we are more likely to follow the 'best hopes' question with 'If you woke up tomorrow to discover that you and your daughter had exactly the relationship you are hoping for, what might be the very first sign?' A side-effect of this less dramatic question, which we have dubbed the 'Tomorrow Question', is that the therapist's words are less memorable, perhaps allowing the client's words to take pride of place. Another feature of the 'miracle' device is that it does not locate power with the therapist. This has its advantage over the commonly used 'magic wand' that tends to be waved by the therapist. 'Let's imagine you wake up tomorrow and your hopes are achieved. What will you begin to notice?' keeps the therapist and the paranormal out of the picture, leaving only the client at centre stage.

38

Distant futures

Sometimes a client might hope for a future that could not begin the next day or even the next year. One teenage boy in a children's home responding to the 'Miracle Question' said he wanted to wake up as a millionaire with a Porsche and a beautiful girlfriend. The therapist responded by saying, 'Let's say the miracle isn't that big and all it does is set your life *moving in the direction* of becoming a millionaire with a Porsche and a beautiful girlfriend'. The boy laughed, told the residential worker to f*** off and went to his room. But the next day, for the first time in several weeks, he rose before midday, bought a local paper, and began looking for a job.

A rule of thumb, though by no means set in stone, is that if the realization of the client's hopes can be located in his or her current life, then waking up with these hopes realized is a real possibility. Feeling confident, an improved relationship, happiness, getting on with life, working hard at school or being a good parent would all be examples of futures that could begin tomorrow. Becoming a millionaire might be more distant, as might finding a partner, getting a new job, passing a distant examination or having a child return from care. In cases such as these, waking up to a future *moving in the direction* of the hoped-for outcome allows for a realistic 'Tomorrow Question'.

39

The qualities of well-described preferred futures: the client's perspective

There are five essential characteristics of a well-described preferred future. First, from the client's own perspective:

1. Positive – something that they want, i.e. what they want *instead* of the problem.
2. Concrete and observable actions – feelings translated into behaviours.
3. Detailed – time, place, actions, context.

And second, through the perspective and actions of others:

4. Multi-perspectival – seen through the eyes of others.
5. Interactional – description of effects on others and vice versa.

1. *Positive.* This is not positive in the optimistic 'glass half full' sense but rather in the mathematical sense of something present, rather than absent. Logically this is obvious – it is not possible to describe something that isn't there. However, we are all prone to describe our hopes in terms of absent problems (I won't be depressed/drink/shout at the children, etc.). The preferred future must describe what will replace the unwanted behaviour or emotion and this cannot be assumed. In one case, a boy in trouble at school said he would no longer run along corridors. It might be assumed that he would walk instead. In fact, when asked by his meticulous therapist, he said he would 'talk to friends', which would require a slowing down. Later, he said he would stop shouting. Again, it might be assumed that instead of shouting he would be talking but when asked what would replace the shouting he said, 'walking' because he would walk over to his friends instead of calling out to them.

2. *Concrete and observable actions.* Clients will most commonly begin descriptions of their preferred future with very broad brushstrokes often involving changed emotional states. For the description to have a therapeutic impact, it needs to be translated into actions. It is not unusual for clients coming for the widest range of reasons – from wishing to overcome heroin addiction to increasing managerial performance – to begin their description with 'I'd feel more confident'. This is an 'inner state' and the client will then be asked how this feeling of confidence will show. Susan, who had come within a literal hair's breadth of suicide (she had cut her thigh down to the artery), said she would open her curtains and answer the door to her worried neighbour; Nina (a heroin addict until the first session) said she would go to the library; and James said he would notice the taste of his breakfast cereal. All three preceded these descriptions with words like 'the first thing I'd notice is that I would want to get up' or 'I'd be looking forward to the day'. However, these descriptions do not immediately tumble off the client's tongue. They need to be worked for with very close questioning.

3. *Detailed.* The more fine detail in the description of the preferred future, the more realistic it becomes. Identifying time and place will add to this sense of possibility. For instance, when a mother is asked what would be the first sign of a good relationship with her daughter being in place, she might say: 'She'd treat me with more respect', to which the therapist might respond, 'What time might that be?' and 'Where are you likely to be when you first bump into each other?' These details will help the therapist to find the right question to produce the beginning of a description of a good and respectful relationship: 'So what might you notice at 8.15 when she comes into the kitchen that gives you the first indication that your relationship with your daughter is as you would like it to be?' – 'She'd say "Good morning, mum", or something like that'.

40

The qualities of well-described preferred futures: other person perspectives

As well as positive, concrete, and observable descriptions, the client's preferred future needs to be fleshed out by two more criteria: the perspective of others and the likely interactions that this future will hold.

4. *Multi-perspectival*. The therapist will not only be interested in the client's perspective of the preferred future but in what others will witness. This is one of the ways in which the client can identify the signs of improved inner states. The mother will know the daughter is feeling respectful when she hears her say 'good morning' and the therapist can then enquire as to what the daughter might then notice about her mother. How family members, friends, colleagues, neighbours, and even passers-by on the street will know that the desired change has taken place will add increasing substance to the description of a preferred future. When a severely depressed person is asked what passers-by might notice if he was feeling how he wanted to feel, he is likely to say things like 'they'd see a man with his head up, maybe catching their eye and possibly even a smile'. This is a description of the small actions associated with a life worth living and as they accumulate they begin to have the potential to bring that life into being.

5. *Interactional*. Finally, it is important that these descriptions are woven into the client's relationships. Not only do we want the observations of others, we want a description of their responses and the effect these responses have on the client. Returning to the mother and her stay-out-late daughter:

Therapist: When she says 'good morning', how might you respond?
Client: I'd say 'good morning' back.

Therapist: And would you be pleased?
Client: Of course I would.
Therapist: How would she know you were pleased?
Client: I'd smile.
Therapist: Would she like that?
Client: I think so, because I think she's as stressed as I am about how things are.
Therapist: How would you know she's pleased?
Client: She'd smile back.
Therapist: And then?
Client: Knowing us there'd be hugs and tears – we'd be so relieved to be speaking.
Therapist: What might be the next thing you'd notice?

It is not the therapist's intention to promote the activity as described by the client. We cannot micro-manage our clients' lives in this way. The aim is just to bring forth a realistic description of the sort of things that *might* happen. The purpose is to create a sense of possibility not to set behavioural tasks. When therapy is successful, the client will report behaviours *like*, but not the *same as*, those described.

41

Broadening and detailing

There are many levels of description and many choices a therapist can make, all of which will achieve their purpose. One decision is when to seek detail and when to broaden the description. With the mother's description of the first 'good morning', the therapist chooses to stay focused on this for several questions. He might have continued this focus by asking, 'As you are hugging and crying, what will you notice about your hopes for the future?' If the client describes another positive feeling, the therapist can ask 'How will your daughter know you have this feeling?' Human relationships are sufficiently complex to spend many more questions on this very brief interchange. At some point, the client has to be helped to move on and broaden the description, usually with a question like 'what else will be different?' It would take too long to give every moment the same level of attention, so the therapist is constantly choosing to 'zoom in' for detail or 'pan out' for breadth.

In the case of the mother and daughter, the therapist begins with detail – the moment of meeting. He might, instead, have begun with a broader description: 'What changes would you like to see in your relationship with your daughter?' The mother might list several, such as more respect, more communication, better reports from school, obedience, and greater signs of happiness. When this wide-reaching description is complete, the therapist can choose where to focus for the detail: 'How would you begin to know that your daughter is happy/showing respect/taking her studies seriously, etc.' As will be seen later, scales can provide a useful framework for eliciting detail across a number of different aspects of a client's life and relationships.

Example

James is 25, well educated but stuck in what he considers to be a dead-end job. He has recently been discharged from hospital after taking an overdose. He lives with his parents who do not get on. His mother is severely disabled by multiple sclerosis and his father works long hours 'to avoid being at home' (according to James, who 'hates' his father). James provides most of his mother's support and this, he says, prevents him from having a life of his own. He would like to have more confidence. This extract is from half-way through the first meeting. James has described getting up, chatting to his mother, being more polite to his father, and more conscientious at work.

Therapist:	And after work, how would your confidence show then?
James:	I'd like to go for a drink but I can't really leave my mother that long.
Therapist:	Would she be upset if you stayed out?
James:	Probably not because she says I should get a life before she dies otherwise I'll be really stuck.
Therapist:	So your mum might even be pleased to see you going out more?
James:	She would if she didn't need me so much or if my dad did more, but he won't because they don't even speak to each other most of the time.
Therapist:	So if they got on better you think your dad might help more?
James:	Yes, but they won't.
Therapist:	If they did, what would be the first sign?
James:	They wouldn't. It's too far gone.
Therapist:	If a miracle happened and they did start to get on, what would be the first sign?
James:	They'd communicate.
Therapist:	About?
James:	Anything and everything.
Therapist:	And what would be the first sign of them just beginning to talk?
James:	He'd help mum more.
Therapist:	What would be the first sign of him helping your mum more?

James:	He'd help her with her oxygen; she needs oxygen now and she can't change the bottle herself, so if I saw dad helping her with the oxygen I'd know they were getting on better.
Therapist:	What difference might that make – seeing your dad change the bottle?
James:	A huge difference.
Therapist:	Like?
James:	Like I'd think I could have a life of my own at long last.

At the second session, a month later, James reports feeling much better, a change of job, and more of a social life. He also reported that his parents seemed to be getting on better with his dad helping out with his mother more. What is likely to have happened is that while James only saw his father as unhelpful, he felt he had to step in. The detailed description probably helped James realize that in his absence the father already did occasional things for his wife and this helped James off the hook.

Part 6

WHEN HAS IT ALREADY HAPPENED? INSTANCES OF SUCCESS

Exceptions

SFBT began with the discovery that nobody is perfect. The new slant on this very old knowledge was that being human we cannot even do our problems perfectly: however chronic, serious, debilitating or complex they are, there are always times when they are less debilitating and less influential on our actions. This phenomenon was best described by de Shazer (1985). He saw problems as repetitive patterns of behaviour, almost like rules, and like all rules subject to exceptions. The notion of *exceptions* is the first pillar of SFBT. The simple equation was that if all problems have exceptions, then all problems have solutions already in place, just waiting to be activated. Early SFBT involved asking about the problem, seeking exceptions, and talking up the exceptions so they grew bigger than the problem.

More easily said than done. Exceptions to problem behaviour generally go unnoticed not least because the problem attracts all the attention. Even when noticed, their significance can be dismissed: a parent or teacher might describe at length a child's naughty behaviour and when asked about good behaviour respond with 'then I know he is brewing something up!' The good behaviour is seen as no more than the beginning of something worse.

The key to making exceptions the basis for change is detail. Once the exception is found, the task is to elicit a detailed description of the alternative behaviour. The more clearly the exception can be described, the more significant its place in the client's repertoire of behaviours. In one instance, a client was so agoraphobic she even had difficulty going near her front door. Eventually, having heard how genuinely frightened this woman was, the therapist asked her how she plucked up the courage to come downstairs each morning as the staircase ended just by the front door. Surprised by the question she went on to describe how each morning was a battle and what she saw as her 'stupid' ways of getting downstairs. Later the therapist asked about her milk delivery, which led to the description of an even more convoluted set of rituals to open the front door so she could have milk for the tea she needed to recover. What the client had noticed about herself over the years in which this problem plagued and curtailed her life was what she saw as her inadequacies. Rather than commend herself for her courage each morning, she berated herself for her weakness. As the interview began to turn the balance, the woman came to see herself in a different light and the problem resolvable because she had been successfully overcoming it every day. Within a couple of weeks she had begun going out by herself, first to the local shop and then further afield until the exceptional behaviour became the 'rule' and the panic an occasional exception.

Since the exceptions-based approach of the early days, there have been significant developments in the practice of SFBT but the central assumption remains: it is impossible to behave with total consistency and however stuck in a problem pattern, there will always be exceptions, times when we do something other than the problem, something that with nurturing has the potential to become a solution.

Instances of the future already happening

Instead of looking for exceptions to the problem, therapists began to seek out *instances* (George *et al.* 1999: 27) when the client's hopes were already being realized. This enquiry turned out to be easier and more efficient than seeking out exceptions, which, when done insensitively, gave the impression that the therapist was suffering from problem-phobia. It also connects the exception/instances more directly to the client's hoped-for outcome.

The interest in what we call instances (of the preferred future already happening) could be said to go back to the development of the 'first session formula task' as described in Chapter 4, where at the end of each first session clients were asked to start noticing what aspects of their lives they wanted to keep. But it was more than a decade before this realization began to play its full part on the solution focused stage.

The difference between an exceptions focus and an instances focus was exemplified in an early case of ours in which parents came with a 7-year-old son complaining of his foul language. Exceptions were successfully discovered and explored and by the next session this was no longer a problem. However, the parents now complained about his poor eating habits. These, too, abated only to be replaced by a further complaint. The therapist was bemused and said he would like to talk to his colleagues before the next session. By then the parents had also given thought to their situation and realized that the problem was theirs. After much soul searching, they had discovered that neither had really wanted children, each having agreed for the other's sake. There was nothing their son could do to please them. They were consumed by guilt and now wanted to shape up as committed parents. Instead of trying, through a focus on exceptions, to put right what was wrong, the therapist began a conversation aimed at working towards a successful future. It soon turned out that despite their hidden reservations, both parents had put more into the task than they were giving themselves credit for and that there was much that they loved about their son once they stopped looking for what was wrong. What they loved about him was in line with their hopes for themselves as parents. The lesson here is that leaving an unwanted place does not necessarily take you to where you want to go; establishing and working directly towards a desired outcome makes for briefer and possibly more effective therapy.

44

Lists

The importance of scales as a way of charting instances of the preferred future will be examined shortly. Another invaluable tool is the *list*. Solution focused interviewing is not an easy process; it is one in which therapists have to search as hard for the questions as their clients have to search for their answers. Whether the search is for exceptions or instances, the greatest fault is to give up too quickly.

The first case of a solution focused therapeutic list illustrates perfectly the importance of persistence. The client was being seen as a routine follow-up by a probation officer who had just completed an introductory course in SFBT and had invited the trainer at BRIEF to supervise his work. The client was a persistent and serious offender not long out of prison and said in a rather blasé fashion that he was now 'going straight'. The probation officer, being new to the solution focused approach, was struggling to develop his powers of persistence. The supervisor suggested he take inspiration from a teaching exercise from the course, in which probation officers were asked to interview each other and find out 35 things that they were each good at in their jobs. So he said, 'okay, tell me 35 things you have done since we last met that are part of "going straight"'. The client began to protest but seeing the officer's determined expression began his list. When, half-an-hour later, he reached his 35 achievement the client was aglow with pride. Long-term follow-up, possible because of his indefinite order, showed him to be living a crime-free life, a life with permanent relationships, job, and contentment. Later he said it was his 35th answer that awoke him to the possibility that change could happen. If the probation officer had been less determined, the outcome may have been very different.

Since then, the creative power of lists has been demonstrated over and over again. Quite why they are so effective remains a bit of a mystery. Sometimes they may be all that is necessary. Daniel came with his mother who was extremely worried that his behaviour at school was going to lead to his exclusion. His home behaviour was also problematic but she thought she could handle this herself. Two weeks after making the appointment, she arrived and said her best hopes were 'for Daniel to sort out his behaviour, though he's doing really well lately, trying really hard, and getting good reports from school'. The therapist asked Daniel what his mother meant and over the next 30 minutes was able to list 20 examples of good behaviour. His mother went on to list another 20 and was then asked: 'If Daniel was doing all these things two weeks ago, would you have asked for therapy?' She laughed and said 'no'. The therapy was over and they had done it all themselves.

In another case, a single teenage mother with learning and physical disabilities was referred because of grave concerns about her capacity (and ability) to be a good enough parent. She admitted to being a poor parent to her first child whom she had at fifteen when she was a homeless heroin addict but was unsure how good she was with her new baby, then six months old. The therapist asked her in what ways she thought she might be a good mother. By the 37th and last answer the young woman had undergone a dramatic physical and apparently intellectual change. She was upright, speaking in a confident and competent tone, and her eyes were bright. One of her last answers had been given with a certain diffidence, as she wasn't sure she would be understood: 'I know my baby can't understand words, I know that but I still can't stop talking to him, but I know he can't understand'. The host of professionals watching over this mother and baby could barely believe the change when she returned from the session. A few months later she was continuing to impress so much that her first child was returned very successfully to her care. Six months after that meeting, a research project was reported in the *Guardian* newspaper saying that children who were spoken to from birth developed faster than others. The therapist sent the article to the client saying 'you got there six months before the *Guardian*'.

Apart from persistence the other aspect of successful listing is to make sure that what is being listed is directly pertinent to the desired outcome of the therapy. Note, however, that lists are used only to derive the instances of the desired outcome already happening; if the client was asked to draw up a list of 35 things they hoped to do in future, the effect of all these to-dos could be to paralyse the client from taking any action at all!

45

No instances, no exceptions

Occasionally, a client will not be able to think of exceptions to the problem or instances of the preferred future already happening or, a little more commonly, that none of the instances or exceptions are significant. These will often be clients so at the end of their tether that the slightest improvement only sharpens the realization of how bad things are. What is most helpful to remember when this happens is that the client is there in front of you. They must be there for a 'good reason' (not just because they were told) and must therefore still at some level have a hope for something different. This hope will be founded on experience even if the client has for the moment lost touch with that experience. Solution focused brief therapists like all other therapists cannot afford to be anywhere but alongside their client. Even though they don't use (and therefore don't seek) information about the problem, they most certainly need to recognize it and to be 'with' their client's pain and misery. To the suicidal client stuck in hospital for almost two years: 'How on earth do you even manage to get up each day?' To the parent who says she has come close to walking out: 'How do you keep going in the face of such rejecting behaviour?' These are not just single isolated questions but entry points to a sequence in which the seriousness of a client's problems will be reflected in a curiosity about how they keep going despite these problems. Most often this will lead to the client becoming more aware of instances and exceptions, those occasional times when life seems more worth living. These 'keeping going' or *coping* questions will be described in more detail in Chapter 55.

Part 7

MEASURING PROGRESS: USING SCALE QUESTIONS

46

Scale questions: the evaluation of progress

As noted in Chapter 5, scale questions have been used from the earliest days of SFBT, and the technique has now been taken up by various therapeutic approaches, including cognitive behavioural therapy. A *solution focused scale* is a way of enabling the client to focus on the degree of progress towards their preferred future; it has nothing to do with assessing the extent of their problem. After a client has explored how they have got to where they are on the scale, they can be invited to consider what will tell them (and others) that they have moved a point further on. It is important to remember that the scale is the client's subjective view of the situation. It is not a scientific assessment!

As we saw in the last section, clients can be asked directly to identify their past achievements. Even when this has been done, it is still valuable to find out what the client thinks of their progress in terms of actually reaching where they want to get to. The therapist can be listening to a client talking about good things they have been managing to do and then be surprised, after asking the scale question, to hear the client say they've only reached 1. This, then, stops the therapist from getting carried away – from the client's point of view, there is still a lot of work to be done. The converse may also be true: the therapist is thinking there's still a long way to go, and the client tells them they're at 9!

For this reason, it is very common for a therapist to go straight from the preferred future part of the interview to a scale. It is strongly recommended that the client is only asked the scale question *after* talking about the future. There is some evidence that clients put themselves higher after the exploration of the preferred future than if they are asked to scale themselves too early, when they are more focused on the problem than on the preferred future.

The simplest form we use is to ask the client to think of a scale where 10 = their preferred future and 0 = the worst it has been for them (some practitioners substitute 1 for 0). Instead of using jargon words to clients like 'your preferred future', it is better to say that '10 stands for all the things you have been saying you want to see different for yourself in future'. It is important to remember that 10 represents the *presence* of the preferred future and not the *absence* of the problem.

47

Designating the '0' on the scale

Designating the 0 takes some thought. In SFBT, unlike other approaches, we are not inviting the client to imagine what the worst could be. So how we refer to the zero is important in keeping the client focused on their progress rather than on their fears.

We can say '0 = the worst it *can* be' (without asking them to elaborate) or '0 = the worst it *has* been'. We are hoping for a response higher than 0 because we want the client to remember useful things and 0 might appear to block that off. 0 responses, rare as they are, will be discussed later on. They can be deliberately avoided by defining the 0 below the client's present position. With a couple seemingly near to separation, for example, 0 could be defined as divorce. In one case where the mother and her 9-year-old son had expressed concern that social services might take the boy into care, the therapist said that '0 is that social services think things have got so bad that they have taken him away'. As this was based on the fear they had already expressed, this made sense to them. In another case, a 16-year-old (seen with his Connexions personal adviser) was told '0 = your mother has thrown you out, and your best friend doesn't want to know you'. The therapist had no evidence that either of these things was possible; he merely intensified what he assumed were the young man's fears. The client acknowledged that that was correct with regard to his mother ('she has already threatened to chuck me out') but then proceeded to correct him that his best friend 'would never not want to know me'. So the therapist removed that from the 0, realizing that he had risked losing the client's trust by his assumption; as it happens, the client gave an answer of 4. So the general rule of thumb seems to be: keep '0' as vague as possible, e.g. '0 = the absolute opposite' (of the preferred future) or define 0 as a generic (and unlikely) worst: '0 = you decide never to get out of bed again'.

A very interesting 0 is to say it represents 'the time you made this appointment'. This encourages the client to think carefully about pre-session changes. de Shazer (2001) suggested clients would put things higher than if they were told 0 represented 'when things were at their worst'.

48

Different scales

In the previous chapter, we dealt with the general, overall scale that is used in almost every solution focused session. There are, however, numerous other scale questions that can be adapted for particular clients.

A 10 represents the achievement of the client's preferred future. In some cases, that future contains many diverse elements. It as if the therapist is mixing them all together; the client's rating is then, in effect, an average of progress towards a number of different preferred outcomes.

For example, a client's 10 in the first session represented living independently of his family, having a job, having driving lessons and getting a car, having a girlfriend, and managing his psychotic illness. In the second session, it seemed that it would be useful to the client to separate out these different components, so the client and therapist engaged in a fine-tuning process of *multi-scaling*, where they examined together each of the goals as a separate scale. These could then be cross-referenced. The result was a significant record of achievement and a realization that the smallest progress on any one scale was likely to have a positive effect on them all.

After the general scale, the most commonly used version is one known as the *confidence scale*. Here the client is asked to rate their confidence on a 0 to 10 scale of achieving their preferred future (or +1 on the scale in a certain time span). The value of this scale is that if someone shows they have some confidence, they can be asked about what gives them that confidence, what they know about themselves (and what others know about them) that tells them there is a chance of progressing. This has the effect of further empowering the client to make changes that are good for them. On the other hand, if the client reveals they have low confidence, this can be taken into account by the therapist, for example by asking the client how they might hope to cope if things *don't* get better. Some therapists find it helpful to assume that if the client says their confidence is below 5, this means there is a good chance progress won't be made, and then coping questions are called for. And then it is possible to ask a *coping scale*: 10 = you couldn't be handling this any better than you are, and 0 = you couldn't cope another minute.

With couples, it can be a powerful intervention for the therapist to ask each in turn to guess what they think the other would say, for example 'where do you think she will say the relationship is now?' (turning to her: 'I'll ask you later what you *do* think'), or 'how important do you think he's going to say making this relationship work is for him on a 0 to 10 scale?' They might think they know what the other is thinking but when they get it wrong, the therapist asks the one with the higher rating what they know that the other doesn't!

Scales are usually talked about in the conversation between practitioner and client, but there are no limits to *how* scales are used. For example, with young people it is often very engaging for them to be able to draw the scale themselves and write where they are now. With younger children, a 'walking scale' can be employed where the scale is 'drawn' from wall to wall (or defined by chairs or cushions) and they walk to the next point up when they have defined the progress already made. With a family, everyone present can write or stand where they see they have got to on the scale, and the worker can add up the 'scores' (or get a child to do it!) and take an average.

49

Successes in the past

'What have you done to get to 3 on the scale?'

The main purpose of the scale is to get at the progress the client has already made. Beginners to solution focus are often in a hurry to get the client to talk about *moving up* the scale. As a general rule, we suggest that they endeavour to find out four things the client has *already done* for every one thing they *might do* in future.

It is not uncommon to hear a client say, 'I'm only at 3' and proceed to give reasons for being this low, often phrased in terms of 'I'm not doing this or that'. There is a temptation for some, especially those with less experience, to want to interrupt the client to say that 3 is really very good and direct them to talk more 'positively'. In these situations it is useful to be reminded of Bill O'Hanlon's advice that we should keep one foot in acknowledgement and one foot in possibility (see Chapter 17; O'Hanlon and Beadle 1996). This means that the client's disappointment or frustration is acknowledged first and foremost. 'So, it seems to you that you are not as high on the scale as you would like because you have lost your temper badly this week. And I'm interested in how come it's 3 and not lower?' If the therapist in this example had said 'but' instead of 'and', the client might have felt that their disappointment was being dismissed, as if they were being told 'it can't be that bad – after all, you're at 3!'

A useful question that can be asked is 'what's the highest you've been on the scale?' The client is expressing their concern that they are 'only' a 3, and yet two weeks ago they were at 6, so they can be asked to say what they were doing when they were at that point. While all and any achievements can be useful to focus on, those that relate to the client's preferred future are of particular value, as they are evidence to the client of their capability of achieving that future. The aim, therefore, is to get as much detail as possible, and using the idea of lists (Chapter 44) can be very useful: 'tell me 10 ways you've got to 3'.

All these questions – How come you're at 3? What were you doing when you were at 6? – are used to increase the client's sense of their own resources and strengths. Various questions help in this endeavour. As in other areas of solution focused interviewing, inviting the client to see herself through the eyes of significant others can be particularly valuable. 'What would your partner/boss/mother say you have done that's been helpful to you? What difference did it make to them that you did those things?'

One way of thinking about the client's responses is in terms of *strategy* and *identity* (see Chapters 63 and 64). When the client is asked what she did to reach 3, these are, in effect, strategies that she could draw on to use in future. When she is asked what it took for her to do that, what it tells her about herself as a person, then these can be seen as identity questions.

A good example of the importance of uncovering past achievements, of enabling the client to notice them and to name them, came in a session with a bright 12-year-old young man with Asperger's syndrome. He found future focused questions very difficult, but enjoyed the scale: in the first session he had carefully written on the scale that he was at 2.5. As each session went by, he was asked where he had got to and how he had managed it. But he found the meetings increasingly difficult: he didn't like being asked so many questions. When he had reached 5, and was being asked as usual about how he had continued his progress, he kept saying 'don't know' and got angry and demanded to know why he was being asked all these questions. The therapist suggested that if he didn't know how he got to 5, then how would he know how to get to 6? He stopped, thought, said 'you're right' and then made more of an effort to give an answer.

50

What is good enough?

'So, you're at 3 on the scale. Where would you have to get to in order to think "that's good enough"?'

There are occasions when the therapist will sense that the client's 10 is unrealistic. In some cases, the client will himself have been referring to his future as the 'perfect' or 'ideal' day. Although it is not recommended that the therapist think about how to make the client's preferred future more realistic – after all it is the client's life, not the therapist's – the therapist might want to do something to 'ground' the conversation. The scale in itself does this wonderfully: however unrealistic their 10 might be, once they say where they are now, the client is thinking 'realistically' and can be encouraged to focus on what +1 will look like (rather than how they are going to get to 10).

An approach that both accepts the client's 10 *and* helps them become grounded is to ask the client where on the scale would be 'good enough' for them to reach. Very rarely do they say it has to be 10! An example was with a client with multiple sclerosis who gave various answers to the Miracle Question that seemed to the therapist likely to be truly miraculous given the nature of her condition. Asked where she was now, she said '2'. This was discussed. Then the therapist asked her where on the scale she would hope to reach to feel she'd made significant progress from the therapy and she said '6'. This, in effect, reduced the scale from 0 to 10 to 0 to 6.

For most solution focused practitioners, the question 'what is good enough?' is used only occasionally, but there are some who choose to ask it every time. They might say 'given nobody's perfect, where would you settle for?'

51

Moving up the scale

'What will tell you you've moved one point up?'

The most important function of the scale, as we have noted, is the opportunity it provides for client and therapist to explore what the client has already achieved and how they did it. Often, this in itself is sufficient to enable the client to work out for themselves what they could do next, especially when the descriptions are very detailed. However, it is common practice to proceed to ask the client how they will know when they have reached one point further up the scale. The focus on one point (rather than the jump to 10) enables the client to specify actions that will tell them and others they are progressing. There is something of a self-fulfilling prophecy about this, as in all future focused interviewing: if the client can detail future actions, they are more likely to notice themselves doing these things later on. However, in the next chapter, we note how it is best to avoid looking for a 'plan of action' from the client.

Some practitioners have taken the idea of list-making and applied it to moving up the scale, as in 'tell me 20 ways you will know that you have moved forward'. We do not recommend this. When clients are asked to specify a list in relation to the future, there is a risk they will experience this as pressure to perform all these actions. We only apply lists to *past* actions, as these represent actions already taken that *might* be repeated in future.

52

Signs or steps

Should one ask, 'what will be the *signs* that you have moved up one point?' or 'what do you need to do to get one *step* higher?'

The beginner is more likely to choose the second question, because it seems more direct: it puts the client on the spot, and often leads to the formation of an *action plan*, whereas the first question is 'softer', more reflective, looking only for signs and therefore doesn't commit the client to any particular action.

Both these approaches are useful and it isn't a case that the therapist must do this or that: some clients will say that an action plan is what they want to go away with, and so the therapist will try to 'fit' with that wish. However, a closer examination of the difference between these questions reveals a considerable difference in approach. We could go as far as to say that the 'signs' question is more true to the solution focused approach than the other.

Harry Korman puts it this way:

> the natural question to ask is: 'What do you need to do to get one step higher?' Once, a young man I was seeing answered this question with 'That's your job, that's why I am here, and do you really believe that I would be sitting here if I knew the answer to that question!!!' I apologised and asked him if I could try another question and he nodded so I asked: 'How will you know that you've gotten one step higher?' He smiled and said, 'You're right. That's a question that only I can answer' . . . responding with what they need to do implies that they should do something – it's none of our business if they do it or not
>
> (de Shazer *et al.* 2007: 64–65)

This seems to get at a crucial principle of the solution focused approach: it centralizes the client's wishes and skills and lets them do the work; it doesn't seek to urge them to any particular course of action. When the client is asked to specify what they *have* to do, it is usually because the therapist is concerned that unless the session ends with some sort of action plan nothing will come out of the work and it has all been just a nice chat. In any case, as Korman has indicated, when asked 'what do you have to do . . .' the client is likely to answer 'don't know', followed by their waiting to hear what the practitioner thinks. Asking 'how would you know . . . and how would others know . . .' leads to more thoughtful processing on the part of the client.

53

What if the client says they are at '0'?

This question is asked at every workshop on the solution focused approach. It is actually a response that clients make only occasionally, but it is a worry for the therapist as to how she should respond were it to happen.

The first thing the therapist should remember is O'Hanlon's mantra (O'Hanlon and Beadle 1996) to *acknowledge* first before moving into *possibility* questions. A little acknowledgement can go a long way. The client's 0 is their way of saying how bad they think things are, and they need to hear that we have heard that ourselves. Beginners sometimes want to rush into trying to make things better, and might respond first off with 'you say it's 0 but look, you got to this session today'. The 'but' implies to the client that you don't think it's as bad as all that. Replacing 'but' with 'and' makes all the difference: 'gosh, that means things must be very tough, and I'm wondering how you managed to get to this meeting today?'

After acknowledging the client's sense of the difficulties they are in, a question that could be asked is 'How come it's not –1?' There is the occasional client who will object – 'I didn't know there were any minuses on this scale!' said one young woman – but generally the therapist can just wait while the client thinks about it.

In a session at BRIEF with a client, a young heroin-using single mother – social services were concerned about the safety of her 2-year-old daughter – de Shazer paused on hearing her 0 response to his scale question (where 0 stood for 'how things were when you arranged for this appointment'), and then asked her 'how come, would you say, that it hasn't slipped below that, down minus one or something like that? How come it hasn't gotten worse?' She said, 'They can't get any worse', to which, after a pause, he said, 'you sure about that?' She looked at her daughter, thought for a moment, and then said, 'well, it could be worse' and then they spoke at length about what she was doing to stop things from being even worse than they were.

Another client at BRIEF, when asked how come she wasn't at −1, said that she would be suicidal in that case, and she knew what that was like because she'd felt that way before. Asked how come she didn't feel that way now, she said it was too awful to contemplate doing such a thing to her son. She was then asked to reflect on how, given the awful relationship she'd described with her own mother, she managed to be a caring mother herself.

In another case, when the client was asked how come it wasn't −1, she answered that it *was* the worst. This then left the therapist no option but to ask 'How will you know you've moved up to 1?', and she proceeded to talk about what she would be telling the social worker, which included the very fact that she had managed to get to the session by herself; the social worker had offered to accompany her.

One should not forget to ask a client who has put themselves at 0 where was the *highest* they have been recently. One client phoned between sessions to say that she had arranged to see her doctor later that day because she was so down, but she was considering not keeping the appointment because she didn't think she could cope any longer and there was 'no point in going on'. The therapist asked her what she hoped for from making the call. She replied, 'Ask me some questions, like the useful ones I get asked in my sessions'. The therapist asked, 'What question would you like me to ask you?' '0 to 10' she responded. 'Okay, so on a scale of . . .' '0!' said the client before he could finish his question. After acknowledging how difficult things must be, and inevitably hearing some more details of what had been difficult for her, he asked her where was the highest she had been in the previous week, and she said '4'. This was when she visited her sister two days earlier. The conversation continued with discussion about what had been different then, and at the end she said she wasn't feeling so desperate, although she still agreed to keep the appointment with her doctor.

54

When the client's rating seems unrealistic

For example, what if a client says, in a first session, that they are at 10? This usually indicates that the client is there against their will. They don't think they have a problem but someone else does – someone who is important or powerful enough to make the client feel obliged to attend. The client is usually hoping that the referrer will 'leave me alone'.

In this case, it makes sense to accept and to hear the client's views as to how come they think they are at 10, and then to explore where they think the other person, usually the referrer, would put them on the scale. After that the therapist would explore what would be a sign to that person that the client was moving forward, and therefore that they were more likely to start to 'leave you alone'.

Sometimes, for similar reasons, a 10 rating may be given in a follow-up session. In a case where the nursery called social services after noticing bruises on a 3-year-old, the father admitted physically abusing his daughter while his wife was out of the country visiting relatives. Their three children were placed in foster care and when mother returned the father agreed to live in a hostel as the condition for the children being allowed to return home. Family work was undertaken to determine whether the father could return home, as he and his wife were requesting, even though domestic violence also came to light. In a session that included the social worker, the family centre worker (who was observing the contact meetings with the children that were allowed to the father), and both parents, everyone was asked to say where they saw things being on the scale, where '10 = the children and the mother are safe enough for the family to be reunited and 0 = as unsafe as things were when the children were taken into care'. The social worker said 5, the family centre worker 6, the mother 8, and the father 10. Everyone's views were taken seriously, and all were asked what +1 would look like, including the father. At the next session, the social worker said things had now reached 6, the centre worker 7, mother 9 . . . and father 20! After some more sessions, father was allowed overnight and then weekend stays with his family. It was some months before he was allowed to move back home altogether.

In another case, the parents had consistently denied the extent of their drinking and their children had been accommodated by social services in a children's home. There was then a major setback for the mother, when she disappeared from home on a drinking spree that nearly killed her. On her return she said she now knew she needed help with her drinking, although the father continued to play down the extent of his own intake. In the next session, the couple appeared looking brighter and cleaner from the therapist's point of view and when they were asked the scale question they both said they were at 10 and asked that the therapist request that their children be returned to them. They said they were only drinking orange juice in the pub. When asked where social services would say things were, they reluctantly said 3. Asked what they thought the social worker would say would constitute signs of progress towards getting their children back, they were, after a while, able to be quite specific: 'we need to go to all the meetings, we need to stop telling the children to break the windows in the children's home . . .'.

A final example. Scott Miller, then working at BFTC in Milwaukee, conducted a session at a substance misuse unit in London where BRIEF conducted live supervision sessions. He was asked to see a heroin-using couple the team had been struggling with. The couple both agreed that they were at 4 on the scale. When he asked them what 5 would be, they said 'to be rehoused'. Those of us watching the session sighed. If this was what it would take for them to reach 5, it was going to be a very long wait! Miller didn't hesitate for a moment. 'What would 4.5 be then?' That led to the couple working harder on what *they* could do.

Part 8

COPING QUESTIONS: WHEN TIMES ARE TOUGH

55

Handling difficult situations, including bereavement

When clients talk about difficult and even traumatic events in their lives, the main source of questions for the solution focused practitioner is linked to what are known as *coping* questions. These were designed by the Milwaukee team to enable clients to look at their skills and strengths for enduring circumstances. This is of relevance whether the client is feeling victimized by voices or anxiety or depression, or someone faced with an external event that oppresses them such as bad housing or experiences of abuse and racism. In the latter case, the therapist may be limited in what they can do to help someone directly with those events but can, perhaps, help the client to deal with things 'at their best'. If, for example, a client is choosing to cope with his circumstances with excessive use of drugs and alcohol, then it might be possible for him to alter that, and questions about when he has most control and drinks less can be very helpful, as well as focusing on ways that he *wants* to cope. More is to be found on the different possible wordings of coping questions in Chapter 66.

In Chapter 33, the point was made that, when a client has been bereaved, it makes sense to explore how they are coping (and maybe have coped with loss before), as bereavement isn't in itself a problem that can be solved. It is also important to check what the client himself wants to talk about. One client came to a session and reported that his father had died in the weeks since the last session. After spending some time hearing about what had happened, the therapist asked what the client was hoping for from the session that day; he said that he would understand that the client might want only to talk more about the loss, and how he was coping. However, knowing the client somewhat, he also wondered if the client wanted to talk about the difference the loss of his father might make to his own future. After thinking for a while, the client said that he'd had a difficult relationship with his father, so despite feeling sad he also felt in some ways free. At the end of the session, the client constructed a plan to go to his father's grave and 'tell' his father about how he was intending to live his life in future.

Coping questions help clients to deal with bad news. Dr. Rob Glynne-Jones, consultant oncologist at Mount Vernon Hospital Cancer Treatment Centre, was conducting an assessment of a 55-year-old patient in the presence of a member of BRIEF. The man had learned only an hour or two before that he had cancer in his jaw and would have to undergo surgery to remove a portion of his face. He was, understandably, numb from the shock of the news. The consultant sympathized with his plight and then gently enquired how the man had dealt with traumatic events in the past. He said that he couldn't imagine that he would have got to the age he had without having dealt with major troubles of one sort or another. The patient thought for a moment and then described how he had managed the death of a particularly close family member. This conversation led to him thinking about how he could prepare himself for the ordeals ahead.

Cancer care is one of the places where solution focused questions are of considerable value in helping terminally ill clients to consider how they would like to live out the remainder of their life. For more ideas, the reader is recommended to consult the work of Joel Simon (2010).

56

Stopping things from getting worse

'What are you doing to stop things from getting (even) worse?'

This is another of the many very useful questions that the Milwaukee team have bequeathed to us. When the client is describing an extremely difficult situation, rather like asking someone who says they are 0 on their scale 'how come it's not –1?', asking this question can enable them to locate their coping strategies. It can also be helpful to explore what they think others who know them would say they do that stops things from getting worse. A client was seen who was an asylum seeker and was sleeping in doorways. He said he was suicidal. He came accompanied by his psychiatric social worker who was asked what she noticed about his way of surviving in such difficult circumstances, and she talked about how he kept all his appointments, was polite to her, tried his best to keep himself clean, and so on. The therapist used this as an opening to explore the client's abilities to do this, even while things were so tough for him.

The client can be asked a confidence scale question (Chapter 48), what they think are the chances that they can continue to stop things from getting worse. As has been suggested before, any low score should be taken seriously as an indication that things may well get worse still and the client would then be asked what options there are for their survival. It may also involve the therapist deciding if there is any action, any duty of care that they should consider, in the interests of keeping the client safe.

Part 9

ENDING SESSIONS

57

Thinking pause

About ten minutes before the end of a solution focused session, many practitioners will take a break for a few minutes – a thinking break. Some of them will leave the room, returning two or three minutes later, while some might stay with their client, in all probability breaking eye-contact, looking down at a pad, jotting down some thoughts for a few moments before continuing. Immediately before this the practitioner will probably have enquired of the client,

> I'm going to take a break in a moment to have a think about the things that you have said and after that I will share some thoughts with you, so just before I do that can I ask whether we have been talking about the right things today? Is there anything else that you had in mind to tell me? Is there anything that I have forgotten to ask and should have or anything that you have forgotten to say?

Assuming that the client says 'no, I think we've been on track – I can't think of anything else that needs to be said', and virtually all clients do respond this way, then the practitioner will take his 'thinking break'.

So what is the purpose of the break? The break originates in the model's systemic, family therapy, history, where it was common for therapists to work with a team placed behind a one-way mirror. About ten minutes before the end of the session, the therapist would withdraw to consult with his colleagues about what to say and what to do at the end of the session. The ends of sessions were seen within systemic therapy to be vital, since this was where the therapy team would formulate their intervention, often focused around a task and for many family therapists this, the delivery of the intervention, was thought to be at the heart of the change process. In addition, from another therapeutic tradition, Ericksonian hypnotherapy, therapists had noticed that on the worker's return the client often seemed to be in a state of 'heightened attention', a trance-like state and thus, they assumed, was more likely to be open to therapeutic suggestion.

Since most solution focused sessions do not involve a team and since thoughts about trance induction are marginal within the solution focused tradition, why is it that workers continue 'taking a break' to collect their thoughts? The answer is straightforward. It is easier to do justice to, and to review, everything that the client has said in fifty minutes of talking if the practitioner is not also trying, at the same time, to listen to the client and to respond. A 'thinking pause' is just what it says: two or three minutes to pull together the key elements of what the client has said during the session that he wishes to include in the session summary at the end.

58

Acknowledgement and appreciation

One of the central themes of Steve de Shazer's thinking that runs throughout his writing is the question of 'expectation'. Early on he stated that 'what seems crucial here is that solutions develop when the therapist and client are able to construct the expectation of a useful and satisfactory change' (de Shazer 1985: 45). The solution focused practitioner is interested in building an expectation, both in the mind of the client and in the mind of the practitioner, that the outcome of the work will be good, that the client will make progress. This intent is reflected in what the practitioner says to the client following the thinking pause.

An example is a case where the practitioner was working with a young man called Paul in his early twenties whose life had been dominated by ill health and by the failure of the medical world to take his conditions seriously. The therapist spoke as follows after the thinking pause:

> Paul, it would be clear to anyone listening to you just how tough things have been for you, not just your struggles with your health, the time that you have spent in hospital, the pain that you have experienced but also the failure of the medical world to get to grips with your situation and to take you seriously. As you said, at times it has felt like living within a never-ending nightmare. And alongside that what has been just as clear has been your extraordinary capacity to keep yourself going, to keep hope alive in your life, to keep struggling and fighting for people to take your situation seriously in order to get the medical treatment that you have needed. And beyond that you have fought determinedly to hold on to your hopes for your life and for your future, you have held on to your wish to be useful to others and even after the recent setback you have been determined to improve your mobility, to be independent again, to live. You

have been going out more, you have been connecting with people again, you have, as you said, been 'living again'. As to the future you are more than clear about your goals for yourself and your best hopes from our talking and you have a very clear picture of the small signs that will tell you that you are moving on from this point that you have already reached. Above all you have '10' confidence that you will progress and that confidence is based on firm evidence.

As is clear from this example there are four key elements to the practitioner's summary:

- Acknowledgement of difficulty.
- Qualities and capacities that the client brings to his life that could be the basis of progress.
- Actions that the client has taken in the direction of the 'best hopes'.
- Signs of hope.

The last three of these are more than clear in the building of expectation but why the first, the 'acknowledgement'? The danger if the worker merely summarizes the evidence of possibility is that the client will worry that the worker has not understood his current position and has underestimated the difficulty facing him. In such circumstances, it would be normal for the client to remind the worker of the extent of the problems. Since this is the very last thing that the solution focused practitioner would wish towards the end of a meeting, a simple acknowledgment of the difficulties tends to reassure the client that he has been understood.

59

Making suggestions

In Chapter 4, in relation to the early history of SFBT, we discussed the centrality of task-setting. Steve de Shazer added to the taxonomy of tasks what he called 'skeleton keys' (de Shazer 1985). These were crucial in the development of his idea that the processes of 'problem formation' and of 'solution development' were distinct, since what they suggested was that a task that was not specifically related to the particulars of the client's problem could nonetheless be associated with change. As noted previously, de Shazer developed the 'First Session Formula Task': 'between now and next time we meet, I would like you to observe, so that you can describe to me next time, what happens in your [pick one: family, life, marriage, relationship] that you want to continue to have happen' (1985: 137). This task can fit with any problem presentation, as can another invention of de Shazer, 'what I would like you to do between now and when we next meet, each time "it" happens, is to do something different' (1985: 122). The task could be applied to almost any 'it' and the 'something' to be done could be anything as well, as long as it was different. Thus de Shazer was enormously interested in tasks, adding to the therapist's repertoire creations such as 'pretend that the miracle has happened', 'structured arguments', 'read-write-and-burn', 'coin-flip' tasks, and prediction tasks or simple noticing tasks.

In its quest for simplicity and the minimization of intervention, the field has moved on and the solution focused world has lost interest in the more exotic interventions that characterized the early days. Many practitioners in their routine everyday practice typically draw almost exclusively on simple 'noticing suggestions': 'between now and when we next meet, what you might like to do is to watch out for the things that you do that take your life in your preferred direction'. The specifics of the noticing must fit with the context of the session and thus make sense to the client, but the key invitation to the client is to move away from a heightened noticing of the problem pattern, which is likely to sustain and to feed it, to noticing the things that they wish to see grow. Solution focus assumes that what we focus on gets bigger.

A further change in the field is exemplified in the shift from the word 'task', or sometimes 'homework', to the term' suggestion'. Prescribing 'tasks' or 'homework' risks creating relational difficulties, since both imply a hierarchical difference. Patients after all cannot *prescribe* for their doctors and school children cannot *set homework* for their teachers. There is also the risk that the practitioner may think that the client who fails to perform the task or the homework is 'resistant', 'unmotivated' or 'non-compliant'. These blaming terms mask the practitioner's part in the failure and limit the likelihood of further progress. However, if the worker 'offers suggestions', a different set of propositions apply. If we offer a suggestion and it is not embraced by the client, we are more likely to turn the spotlight back on ourselves and to ask 'what was wrong with my suggestion' and 'how can I frame a better suggestion next time' or 'is this someone who would get on better without suggestions'. This way of approaching the client's 'failure' to follow through fits with de Shazer's proposition that whatever the client is doing is the best that they can do right now. and it is the practitioner's job to cooperate with what ever the client is doing.

60

Making the next appointment

One of the challenging characteristics of the solution focused approach for practitioners is the extent to which the approach genuinely centralizes the client's preferences and treats the client as 'knowing best'. This applies not only to the construction of the contract, to the assumption that the client's best way of moving forward will be the best way, but also to the process of the therapy. It is the client who is assumed to know best when to finish the work and the client is assumed also to have a legitimate view as to if and when it will be best to meet again. So does this mean that the solution focused practitioner will be prepared to see a client every day, indefinitely, if that is the client's preference? And the fact that the clear answer is 'no' to that question requires us to acknowledge the complexity of the professional role. The structure of the contact is not solely determined by the client's preferences – the professional is also influenced by ethical and 'job description' factors. It is simple to see that a client's expressed preference for further sessions might conflict with the worker's contract to offer just six sessions and no more. However, what if the client elects to continue working with the practitioner and the practitioner is not convinced after perhaps four or five meetings that the work is making any difference or indeed is likely to make any difference? In such circumstances, and after discussion and consideration, the practitioner if still unconvinced of the utility of the work is likely to base their decision to cease on ethical considerations: 'Irrespective of your preferences I do not believe that it would be right to carry on offering appointments, since it seems to me that this risks wasting your time and money'.

In the same way, the arranging of the next appointment is not absolutely straightforward, since many solution focused practitioners take the view, based on their experience, that longer gaps between sessions are often more useful than shorter gaps. Longer gaps give the client time to do something different and thus increase the likelihood that upon their return they will be in a position to report progress. The length of the break will also depend on the client's position, since after all it is evident that people in crisis will have less capacity to stay connected to the work of the session over a longer period of time than those who are aware that they are making progress and for whom the acute crisis is in the past.

These factors resolve in practice into a two-part proposition offered to clients at the end of solution focused meetings. First, 'Do you think that it would be useful for you to come back or would you prefer to have a think about that and let me know?' And if the client elects to have another session, 'So when do you think that it would be best to come back – in two weeks' time, three weeks, less than that or more than that?' This formulation implies that coming back the following week, a process into which many clients have been trained is not necessarily the best. It also ensures that if clients come back, it will be each time on the basis of their decision that a further meeting will be of use to them, rather than on the basis of a predetermined contract. The client is returning because they want something from the session.

Part 10

CONDUCTING FOLLOW-UP SESSIONS

61

What is better?

de Shazer (1987: 60) wrote that 'if you want to get from point A to point B, but know no details of the terrain in between, the best thing to do is to assume that you can go from A to B by following a straight line'. And the straightest line when opening a follow-up session, if we assume that therapy is about constructing changes in people's lives, is to ask the client 'what has been better since we met?'

The use of this question represents a challenge to many therapists who prefer the less defined and less focused question, 'so how have things been since we last met?' Asking how things have been is a question that fits well with a more exploratory, more discursive model of therapy but solution focus, in a benign way, is not interested in people's lives and how people are. It is focused very precisely on the construction of a 'progressive narrative'. de Shazer stated that 'solution-determined (progressive) narratives are more likely than complaint-centred narratives . . . to produce transformations and discontinuities' (de Shazer 1991: 92). The question 'what has been better since we met' serves to focus the client's attention, to direct the client's noticing in a very specific way and not infrequently after one or two follow-up sessions, each of which the worker opens with the same question, the client will comment: 'I knew you were going to ask that so I've been watching out'. Watching out for what has been better is very specifically at the heart of the solution focused change process.

The simple fact that the worker has opened the session in this way does not always, as we shall see, determine the client's response. Some clients will respond with 'nothing, it's the same' and others with 'nothing, in fact things have got worse recently' so clearly that the practitioner needs flexibility in responding even if her opening question is always the same.

62

Amplifying the progress made

Imagine for a moment that when asked by the practitioner 'what has been better since we met?' the client responds by saying 'not a lot really'. The practitioner notices that the client has not answered 'nothing' and that therefore the chance remains that something is better, and it is this story of improvement that the practitioner will be wishing to amplify and to develop.

Therapist:	So what has been better since we met?
Client:	Not a lot really.
Therapist:	Not a lot – so what has been better, even a little?
Client:	Well as I said, not much but on Wednesday I did manage to get out of the house.
Therapist:	Okay – and it's been a while since you've managed that?
Client:	Yes, it has been weeks and weeks, apart from going to the doctor.
Therapist:	Right – so how tough was it for you to get yourself out?
Client:	It was really difficult. I didn't think that I could do it and whenever I saw one of them, I really really wanted to just turn back and go home.
Therapist:	And yet you didn't?
Client:	No, I didn't – I made myself walk all the way to the Nursery, and wait outside and collect Hannah and walk slowly home with her rather than rushing straight back.
Therapist:	Okay – quite an achievement?
Client:	Yes – I even stopped to talk with her friend Sophie's mum.
Therapist:	Okay. So let's go back to the beginning. How did you get yourself out of the front door?

Client:	I just told myself, 'you can't go on ringing mum every day at the last minute to take her to nursery and then to collect her again'.
Therapist:	Sure – and I guess you have said this to yourself before. How come this time you did something different?
Client:	I'm not sure – I talked with mum about it last night . . .
Therapist:	And I guess that you've done that before too? So how come this time you took your own advice and managed to get yourself out of the house and all the way to nursery?
Client:	I'm not sure – maybe I am beginning to feel a bit better.
Therapist:	Right – so what are you noticing that is telling you that you are feeling even a little better?
Client:	Well, I am thinking less about it and what happened.
Therapist:	Right – so you are thinking less about it. How are you managing that? Can't be easy.
Client:	No, it's not easy, but I have decided, not just for me but for Hannah too, that I can't let our lives be ruined by that bastard. I am not going to let that happen.
Therapist:	You're not going to let that happen.
Client:	No, I'm not – he's not worth it.
Therapist:	You sound very determined.
Client:	Yes, I am determined now – and I'm angrier than I was.
Therapist:	Right – so what difference is that making to you feeling angrier?
Client:	It is making me stronger – it is giving me the strength to do things – to face things.
Therapist:	And is that good for you 'doing things' and 'facing things'?
Client:	Yes it is – and I need to do more of it.

This short conversation illustrates the constructing with the client of a new narrative, a story that fits with the likelihood of further change. A small event, getting out of the house to collect her daughter, is gradually seen as being of greater and greater significance. In the next two chapters, we will look at some of the questions that support this shift.

63

Strategy questions

When clients make changes, often only small ones at first, it can be hard for them to attach significance to those changes. The progress they have made can be written off as flukes or indeed the progress can be attributed to others. When the changes are trivialized in this way, when the potential meaning contained within the events is minimized, then the likelihood of more change is reduced. So how do solution focused practitioners move with clients out of the language of chance into a description of active agency? In making this shift, SFBT draws on two types of questions, 'strategy questions' and 'identity questions'.

The most straightforward question available to the practitioner is simply 'how did you do that?' For example, imagine a client reporting to the worker that that very day she had got up, got dressed, and gone out for a walk. Following an opening along the lines of 'sounds like you were pleased to be able to do that', if the client responds in the affirmative, the worker can just ask, 'so how did you get yourself to do that?' Inserting the 'get yourself' into the question implies that it was not easy for the client to do this and any answer that the client gives is likely to point towards self-appreciation, as in 'I dunno, just made myself I guess'. While this answer is potentially a part of a progressive narrative as previously discussed, it is unlikely to be the endpoint of the therapist's curiosity. 'So how did you make yourself?' invites further exploration, further focused thoughtfulness on the part of the client. An easy way for the therapist to invite the client into a more detailed description of the achievement is simply to say, 'tell me 10 things that you did that helped you to get yourself up and out'.

On occasions, clients will not have considered themselves to have played an active part in the outcome and will say 'I don't know – I just felt better'. The solution focused practitioner will still persist: 'so what do you think that you might have been doing recently that is associated with you feeling better?' or 'imagine a video camera had been filming you this morning, following you around the house, what would the film show that you did that ended up with you leaving the house and going for a walk?' If the client still responds by saying 'nothing, I didn't do anything, it just happened', the therapist might ask 'so what did you do to have it just happen?' or 'if you had wanted it *not* to happen, what would you have had to do to stop it happening, what would you have had to think to make sure that you ended up staying at home in your chair?' (followed by questions exploring how come they *didn't* do those things).

The power of strategy questions can be enhanced by the introduction, if appropriate, of the perspective of significant others: 'what do you think those who know you best noticed you doing?'

As the therapist asks strategy questions, the client is not only invited to congratulate herself for her success but is also invited to specify what in particular she did that was associated with the success. The more that the client does this, the more repeatable the success potentially becomes. Even when the client concludes that she really does not know what she did, the effect of these questions is likely to be benign. Having clients puzzle over what in particular they have done that has worked for them is normally strengthening and can be the basis for a collaborative end-of-session noticing suggestion.

64

Identity questions

It is virtually impossible for human beings not to reach 'identity conclusions' about those with whom they interact and indeed about themselves. Human beings are 'sense-makers'. We seek to make our worlds more manageable through the twin processes of observation and categorization. A teacher notices a child being difficult in his class and deals with the incident. The next day, the child behaves badly again and in addition a colleague comes up to the teacher and mentions that the same child has been rude in her class as well. Very soon the teacher moves from the framing 'he *behaves* badly' to 'he *is* a difficult student'. And this shift has significant consequences. Once the child is framed as difficult, the framing itself will serve to make difficult behaviour more visible and good behaviour less so. When we have reached a conclusion we tend to notice those things that confirm the conclusion and once we have reached a conclusion about ourselves, it is subsequently easier for us to act in line with the description and harder to act in ways that contradict the description.

So solution focused therapists ask questions that invite clients into possibility descriptions, ways of thinking about themselves that fit with the greater likelihood that they will be able to achieve their goals for their lives and the work. How is this done? The solution focused therapist will listen for the client to describe an achievement, anything that he has done that is in line with the best hopes from the work. Having elicited a description of a fitting event and having asked one or more strategy questions, the therapist will then invite the client to notice and name the associated qualities, strengths, skills or competencies.

- What did it take to do that?
- What did you draw on to make that change in your life, what strengths, what qualities?
- What does that teach you about the person that you are and the person that you can be?

Any one of these simple questions invites the client to develop a possibility focused description of self: 'it tells me that I am stronger than I realized', 'I had to be really strong', 'it took determination and willpower'. The therapist can then build on these responses. 'Have you always known that you could be that strong?' and if the client responds by saying 'no' the therapist can enquire, 'so what difference will it make to your future, knowing that you can be that strong?' If the client replies by saying that strength has always been a part of his life, the worker can highlight that capacity by asking: 'tell me about other times in your life when you have been strong'.

Asking questions in this way, inviting the client to 'notice and name' his own qualities, is very different from the therapist telling the client. Over-enthusiastic therapists can often be tempted to tell – 'you come across as a very determined person' – risking disagreement on behalf of the client. People frequently doubt apparent compliments coming from the mouths of others, but are much more likely to believe the things that they hear themselves saying. Invitations to self-compliment rather than praising are characteristic of this approach.

65

When the client says things are the same

Just because the therapist asks 'what's better since we last met?' does not guarantee a positive response from every client. Some will respond 'nothing, absolutely nothing has changed, it's exactly the same'. Although by the end of the session the client may have noticed that some things are indeed better, it is best for the solution focused therapist not to argue, 'come on something *must* be better', and to work from the position of accepting that the client means exactly what she says. If we argue, we risk merely inviting the client back into reiterating the statement 'nothing is different', and each time the client repeats this, the harder it is for the client to notice that this might not be completely so.

Therapist:	So what's been better since we last met?
Client:	Nothing – absolutely nothing has been different – it's exactly the same.
Therapist:	Oh. So what have you been pleased to notice about the way that you have been going about things, even though nothing is better?
Client:	Well, I suppose just that things have not got worse either.
Therapist:	So, could I ask you a few questions about that – what do you think that you might have been doing to stop things getting worse?
Client:	Well – I have carried on paying attention to my diet and looking after myself a bit better, getting to bed at a reasonable time, sleeping okay and getting out a bit.
Therapist:	Okay – so those are things that one way or another you have managed to maintain?
Client:	Yes I have.
Therapist:	So how have you managed to keep those good things going?

Client:	Just making them into a habit – a bit of a routine really – making myself do them even when I don't feel like it.
Therapist:	I imagine that that cannot be easy – making yourself do things when you don't feel like it – so how have you managed that?
Client:	Just remembering what it was like last year.
Therapist:	Okay – so one way or another you have managed to keep things going and it sounds like that isn't easy.
Client:	No.
Therapist:	So how will you know when the time is right to take another step forward, to move things on again?
Client:	Not sure.
Therapist:	How do you think?
Client:	Maybe when it doesn't feel like a struggle every day.
Therapist:	Okay – so how will it be feeling?
Client:	Bit less on a knife edge – bit less like I could fall off at any time.
Therapist:	Okay, great – so if you're not quite so much on the knife edge what will you be instead?
Client:	More confident – more confident of the future.
Therapist:	So what will you be noticing about the way that you are going about things that will allow you to be more confident?

It is clear from this extract that at no point does the therapist argue with the client. The therapist accepts the client's response and by asking 'so what have you been pleased to notice about the way that you have been going about things, even though nothing is better?', the client moves into detailing an alternative achievement and the conversation can then focus on what the client has done in the service of stabilization. Asking the client towards the end of the extract 'how will you know when the time is right to take another step forward, to move things on again?' builds the basis for a beautiful collaboration, paced at the client's pace.

66

When the client says things are worse

There will be a time when every solution focused brief therapist asks, 'so what has been better' and the client will answer 'you're joking surely, it's been worse, ten times worse. This week has been just about the worst week of my life'. While it can be tempting for the panicky practitioner to try to trick the client out of his position 'but you got yourself here – how did you manage that?' with the underlying logic 'if things were really so bad you wouldn't be here, but you are here so it cannot be that bad', this approach is always worth resisting. Clients resent therapists' refusal to accept what they are saying, so a much simpler start is, 'I'm really sorry that you have had such a tough time'.

Once the client feels acknowledged and accepted, the therapist can begin the task of searching for a way of connecting the conversation to the direction in which the client wants to move, to something that fits with the likelihood of the client being successful.

It sounds like this last fortnight has been really tough for you, and things have even gone backwards if I understand what you are saying. So:

- What have you been pleased to notice yourself managing to get done despite all the difficulties?
- How have you managed to keep hope alive at all in your life given the setback you have faced?
- How have you kept yourself going at all in the face of all the problems you have had to deal with?
- What have you done to stop things getting even worse than they have already – how did you stop the slide here?

Each of these questions could open a pathway towards a purposeful conversation, focusing on what the client has done that is of use to him. And each question in this situation needs to be sufficiently acknowledging of the client's situation for the client to feel prepared to respond. If the client feels that the questions fail to recognize the gravity of his situation, he will be tempted back into problem description and then the therapist will need to incorporate a greater recognition of difficulty into his question to re-establish the fit. In the process, the therapist risks inviting the client effectively to detail yet more of the problem.

Therapist:	Sounds a nightmare.
Client:	Yes it has been.
Therapist:	So, how have you been coping?
Client:	Well that's just the point – I haven't been coping. I'm finding it hard to get up, I'm not getting dressed, I've started drinking again, and Eileen says that if I go on like this she is off.

It is clear that the question 'so how have you been coping' is just too 'functioning' a description of life to work for the client, and as a result the client moves back into detailing the difficulties. If the therapist had substituted a less 'functioning' description, perhaps 'so how on earth have you been getting through at all given just how tough things have been', the client may have felt sufficiently validated to accept the therapist's invitation. As Steve de Shazer used to say in public presentations, 'we may be solution focused but we're not problem-phobic'. When therapists become 'problem-deniers', their work becomes solution forced and it is clear that solution forced work does not work (Nylund and Corsiglia 1994).

Part 11

ENDING THE WORK

67

Maintaining progress

Many approaches to counselling or therapy see the process of 'ending' as highly significant, as something that needs to be managed or to be 'worked through' over a number of sessions. In solution focus, this careful attention does not seem to be necessary and most endings are relatively informal, with clients often saying that they see no need for further sessions right now but that they will get back to the therapist if the time comes when a further review of the situation would be useful. The reasons for the difference are clear. First, the typical number of meetings between therapist and client is less than four and these meetings may have taken place over a period of 10 weeks with relatively long gaps between the meetings. Even in this very real way the therapist will typically remain tangential in the client's life, but in addition the therapist will work hard to maintain a marginal position, with the client and her life centralized in the process. As a client of Chris Iveson's spontaneously said, 'Do you know Chris when you ask good questions you disappear – it is only when you ask bad ones that I notice you' (George *et al*. 1999: 35). Insoo Kim Berg echoed this theme, the marginality of the therapist in the solution focused approach, in her statement that the worker should aspire to 'leave no footprints in the client's life'. Indeed, the approach values this 'invisibility', holding the view that change is better maintained by clients when the client takes the credit for the changes made rather than the client 'crediting' the worker for the changes, as in 'I couldn't have done this without you' (Sundman 1997). Thus it is clear that in SFBT, by and large, the figure of the therapist remains of marginal significance, merely asking questions from the edge of the client's life and at the end of the session summarizing back to the client some of the things that the client herself has said.

In some circumstances, the therapist may focus more directly on finishing, most often when the therapy is becoming more prolonged, by asking 'let's imagine that you woke up this morning and just knew that there was no need for us to meet again – what were you noticing that told you that further sessions were not necessary?' This question serves to re-specify the outcome and refocus, if necessary, the work to thinking about what needs to be achieved for a consensual ending to be possible. However, in addition it can be useful for the worker to ask the client, 'On a scale of 0 to 10 with 0 standing for you having no confidence whatsoever in your ability to maintain the progress that you have made and 10 standing for you being completely confident in your ability to do so, where would you put yourself at present?' The therapist can further emphasize ending, especially with a client low in confidence of maintaining progress, by asking, 'and where would you need to be to feel ready to end our talking together?' and then 'so how will you know that you have reached that point?'

68

What if there is no progress?

Nothing always works. However talented the worker and however useful her approach, there will be times when there is no report of change on the part of the client, when each session elicits the response 'nothing's better', and when there is never a shift in the client's position on their 'best hopes' scale. In such circumstances, the third rule of SFBT comes into play: 'if it doesn't work, do something different' (Chapter 10). So what can the therapist do in these circumstances that may make a difference?

1. Check the client's 'best hopes' from the work and invite the client to scale the possibility of achieving those hopes. 'On a scale of 0 to 10 with 10 standing for you just knowing that you can make this change and 0 standing for the opposite of this, where would you put things?' If the response is very low, it is possible to renegotiate the best hopes.
2. Invite the client to try a 'being bothered' scale – how much, in other words, does the achievement of the 'best hopes' matter to the client. If the response is low, the therapist can seek to renegotiate the 'best hopes'; if high, the therapist can build on the response by scaling how much the client is prepared to do: '10 I would do anything to make progress with this, 0 nothing'.
3. Change the make-up of the session – if working with a family or couple, meet with the individuals separately; if with an individual, invite the client to bring someone else.
4. Meet the client at a different time of day or in a different place.
5. Change the therapist.
6. Evaluate with the client the progress made, or the lack thereof, and ask the client for his advice on what the therapist could do differently.

7. Ask a colleague to offer a live consultation to you and to the client, interviewing you both in the presence of the other and observing what emerges from the talking that is useful.
8. Change approach, either drawing on an alternative approach that the same worker is competent in or seeking an alternative therapist using a different way of working.

If after all this nothing changes, then the question remains why the therapist should carry on working with the client when nothing useful is happening. Agreeing to see a client where there is no change risks confusing and misleading the client, inviting him to think that he is addressing the difficulty when in fact nothing of use is emerging. In this way, the therapist can become a part of the problem stabilization system. Refusing to carry on at least opens the possibility that the client will be challenged to 'do something different' and whatever it is that the client does holds the possibility of a shift. An alternative is to suggest, or agree with the client, that now may not be the right time to make changes in his life and that instead the time may be right for stabilization and only when the client knows that he is ready to take the next step should the client return to the therapist.

Part 12

ASSESSMENT AND SAFEGUARDING

69

Assessment

Traditional therapies have typically initiated the therapeutic process with two areas of assessment, prior to any thought or question of intervention. The first area of assessment examines the question of the client's fitness for therapy, seeking to determine whether the client is the sort of person who can be helped with a 'talking cure'. This might involve exploring, among other things, the client's cognitive capabilities, their ability to articulate, and maybe their theory of causation and how that fits with the delivery of a psychological intervention. In addition, the traditional therapist will seek to explore the nature of the problem, perhaps developing a hypothesis regarding problem causation and maintenance, and then considering whether the defined problem is amenable to the therapist's specific model of intervention or posing the question, 'which model would best help this particular client'.

Within SFBT there is no pre-therapy assessment phase. Since it is assumed that every client is doing the best that he can at the time, it is the job of the therapist to determine whether she can find a way of satisfactorily fitting with the client's best, and this is a question that can only be determined in the therapeutic process itself. In addition, nothing within the outcome research to date gives us any way of knowing for whom this approach is useful and for whom it is not, in terms of demography, client presentation or indeed in terms of the problem that the client brings (see Chapter 12). Each solution focused intervention thus becomes essentially an experimental process with at its heart the question, 'Can I as a therapist find a way of fitting with this client's presentation sufficiently usefully for something different to be generated, a difference that will make a difference?' Thus the questions that the solution focused therapist poses herself are 'therapy process' related rather than focused on the client's inner world and how that is being manifested in the interaction between client and therapist. The therapist is not trying to 'understand' the client, to evaluate the client's behaviour or to work out what, in lay language, makes them tick. The idea is to stay as much as possible 'on the surface' rather than trying to look behind and beneath.

So the therapist in the solution focused approach asks her first question, then listens to the client's answer, and attempts to shape a question that takes account of the answer *and* moves the conversation in the direction of possibility. And so on and so forth. To this point the therapist is focused on the narrative, the content; however, there is another process that takes place in a parallel fashion centred on the question 'is this working?' or perhaps 'is the client coming with me in this conversation?' If the client is collaborating with the therapist's attempts to collaborate with the client, then the therapist will proceed on the basis of de Shazer's second rule 'if it works, do more of it' (Chapter 10). But if the client is not moving with the process, then de Shazer's third rule – 'if it is not working, do something different' – takes precedence and the therapist needs to make adjustments to the process. Perhaps the pacing is wrong, maybe the client wants to tell more of her problem story. Perhaps an 'other person perspective' question will allow the client to see himself in the future rather than being invited to see the future through his own eyes – 'how will your best friend know that you coming here has been of use to you?' Maybe for a client who is finding it hard to move away from her problem description an exception question might work better than an instance question, or maybe focusing on the client's managing, even nearer to the problem experience, would work better. The skilled solution focused therapist listens to the content of the client's response and simultaneously evaluates 'fit'. On this basis, they draw on the full range of solution focused responses and judge which response offers the requisite sufficient fit with the client's position to make sense to the client and sufficient distance from the client's position to introduce the possibility of change (Andersen 1990).

70

Safeguarding

The authors began their solution focused careers while working at the Marlborough Family Service, a specialist NHS clinic providing (among other things) assessment and treatment of families with children at severe risk of harm. Their early solution focused practice was partly built around this work (George *et al.* 1999). It was apparent that a solution focused approach had much to offer in promoting safety. It was equally apparent that like any other therapy model, it could not be used alone as an assessment tool. Assessment and treatment might inform each other's processes but always need to be seen as separate activities.

Andrew Turnell has done pioneering work in this area, with the 'Signs of Safety' model now being adopted by safeguarding services around the world (Turnell and Edwards 1999). In essence, the model provides a simple grid on which to chart both the risk and the safety factors in a situation. Only when there is a balance in favour of safety, or the possibility of safety, do therapeutic or change-directed conversations take place. At this point, SFBT has much to offer. Attention to what the client is already doing well (e.g. 'What do you think you already do well as a parent?') serves to boost collaboration and confidence and this is further enhanced when the therapist begins to seek out the client's own hidden skills: 'If you woke up tomorrow morning exactly the parent both you and social services would like you to be, what might be the first thing you would notice?'

SFBT has also been effective in reducing domestic violence (Lethem 1994; Lee *et al.* 2003). By focusing on safety and how it can be promoted, victims of violence are able to bring more of a sense of control into their lives without implying they somehow share responsibility for the violence against them. As an example, Josephine has been describing a 'tomorrow' in which she had got her 'self-respect' back. She has a cut above her left eye and because the police have notified social services of this attack on her by her baby's father, she is at risk of her newborn being removed from her. In the process of describing a safe future, her voice has grown stronger, she is sitting more upright, and is no longer sure that she has brought 'all this' on herself. On a 'safety scale' she is at 4. After a lengthy focus on what she is already doing to help keep herself safe in this dangerous environment, the therapist asks: 'What might be different at 5 on the scale?' Josephine says that she will have her keys back and this will give her more of a sense of control (even though she knows her ex-partner can kick down the door). Exploring what a greater sense of control might lead to, Josephine talks of going out more ('I don't even go to the supermarket anymore!') and reconnecting with friends. These are such obvious routes to safety but they usually only become viable routes when the client discovers them for herself. Otherwise, it is just another 'powerful' person telling her what she should do. Asking how being more in touch with friends might impact on her safety, Josephine comes up with the idea of going to see her ex with the friend who introduced them: 'He'll never do anything in front of her'.

Over nine months and seven sessions Josephine was never hit again. She stayed in an on–off relationship with the same man but on very different terms. As she was saying goodbye at the end of the work, she asked: 'Did I ever tell you I was anorexic?' To the therapist's 'No' she responded, 'Well I'm not anymore, so thank you for that too!'

Part 13

CHILDREN, FAMILIES, SCHOOLS, AND GROUPWORK

Children

People are often surprised about how very young children can respond to SFBT. Mostly, however, a therapist will choose to work with parents rather than children, as there is always the chance that by being identified for individual work a child will pick up an unhelpful label and be assumed to be problematic. Assumptions like this can devastate a child's life. Furthermore, if a parent rather than a therapist can be credited with success, the change is likely to have more sticking power. If a child is to be involved, he or she will need to have reached the developmental stage at which difference can be discerned, most commonly by the age of three when they are able to stack toy bricks and thus create a rudimentary scale.

The main difference when working with children, and this will be true of any therapy, is that the language needs to be adjusted – the child needs to understand and be able to answer the questions. The younger the child the less abstract the questions will need to be, and the emphasis may need to be more on the actual past than on the imagined future. Words might also be supplemented by materials and play (Berg and Steiner 2003). A 5-year-old will usually enjoy demonstrating 'good behaviour' at school, especially if joined by whoever else is in the meeting, by showing how he can first sit quietly, then line up quietly, and finally walk quietly. He might never have been seen to do this before but he is very likely to start doing it the next day after such a demonstration. One such 5-year-old said that for things to be happier in school he shouldn't run in class. He was asked what he should do instead. 'Walk', came the reply. 'Are you a good walker?' asked the therapist. 'Yes!' he replied emphatically. 'Good', said the therapist, 'show me how', and with that the boy took a slow and measured turn around the therapy room, demonstrating for the therapist and his mother his considerable skill. Later in the session he engaged with the therapist in a role-play, where he took the role of the teacher and the therapist that of the child himself, so that he could 'teach' the therapist what was required of him as the child!

In another case, an elective mute 4-year-old was able to illustrate her current level of safety by choosing one from a line of ten plastic farm animals. Then using pipe cleaner dolls she indicated that it was a mixture of her mother's proximity and her father's attention to her brother (who had raped her) that was keeping her safe. After being helped to communicate in this way she began to speak again. In another case, a very active boy enjoyed comparing his aims and progress towards them with skateboard manoeuvres. Both his skateboarding and his behaviour began to improve.

Apart from language, the most obvious difference with smaller children is in establishing their hoped-for outcome. Often this will be largely determined by parents but a child can be included and 'informed' of the benign nature of the therapy by being asked questions such as: 'Would you like to be happier/get on with your brother/behave well at school', etc. These are examples of 'closed' question that can be answered with a single word (like asking a child the name of their favourite TV programme), and is therefore easier for children to answer and enables them to feel they are 'getting it right'. The therapist can then switch to 'open' questions, which cause the child to have to think harder before giving an answer: 'Okay, so, let's say tomorrow you have a happy day in school, how will Miss know you're happier when you come into the class? What will she see you doing?'

Adolescents

Some practitioners, even highly experienced ones, find the idea of working with adolescents daunting. They fear the constant 'don't know' responses, the apparent lack of engagement, the battle to draw their eyes away from their mobile phones and their ears from their headphones. SFBT provides a very constructive framework for work with adolescents. They appreciate the focus on the future and the emphasis on concrete descriptions of actions (Lethem 1994). Most importantly, SFBT centralizes *their* views. It is also time limited, and this goes for the length of sessions as well: half an hour is often more than enough.

The 'don't know' response that is heard so often from young people doesn't have to be a worry. At times, it resembles a sort of default response, as if the client says it without thinking and *then* stops to consider whether to answer the question. All that is required of the practitioner is persistence to show that one really wants to hear their answer: 'What do you think?' 'What's your guess?' If these open questions draw a blank, then it might be best to start with a closed question before moving on:

Therapist:	It seems that things have been difficult lately, is that right?'
Client:	Yes.
Therapist:	And you would like things to go better?
Client:	Yes.
Therapist:	So let's say things *did* go better, what would you notice?

For some young people, especially those who feel they have been sent against their will, it is useful to ask them what a third party is hoping to see different. For obvious reasons, questions relating to their friends are immensely useful for adolescents. One 14-year-old young woman who kept saying 'don't know' when asked about what she wanted from the work responded to 'What would tell your friends that this hadn't been a waste of time?' with 'I wouldn't be so unhappy'. Upon being asked 'How will they know that?', she said: 'I'd talk more to them'.

Scale questions of various kinds are much appreciated. One 16-year-old (see Chapter 47) who never saw the mornings spent most of his time smoking 'weed' and was under threat of being thrown out by his mother. When asked the scale question, he remembered that two days previously he had cleaned half the house. He put this down to boredom, but was able to think about the benefits it had led to such as a reward from his mother, and how he could go on to make further progress.

One of the more useful questions is the *coping* question. Young people have to endure (as they see it) so much from the adult world, as well as from peers and sometimes from their own emotions and changing bodies. Asking 'How do you handle that?' ensures that the client feels that their struggle is being acknowledged, and enables them to explore their skills in managing their lives. They may be engaging in self-harm or excessive use of alcohol or substances, and there may be a place for discussion about the risks involved if the client appears to be truly ignorant of the consequences. But questions that relate to how they control those activities, on the assumption typical of solution focused work that there will be times when they resist the urge to go to excess, will lead to questions about other, safer, ways they have of managing their lives.

While the *strategy* questions (Chapter 63) of SFBT are a perfect fit for young people, *identity* questions (Chapter 64) are often of great value. Adolescents are acutely concerned with questions relating to their identity, their reputation, and how they are perceived. There is, in short, something in SFBT for all adolescents.

73

Family work

Although it is not necessary for all family members or both partners of a couple to attend for change to happen, very often there will be more than one person in the room.

So what happens if family members differ about the preferred future?

Let us take the most obvious and simple example, a parent and an adolescent. The likelihood of the two agreeing about their best hopes, certainly at first, is minimal. Many parents express the hope that their child will 'show more respect' and by that very often they mean that the child will be obedient. The young person, on the other hand, expresses a wish for 'trust' and by that they normally mean that they will be allowed more freedom. Looking backwards is likely to lead to fruitless tit-for-tat dispute: 'How can I trust you when you don't come home all night?' 'How can I respect you when you treat me like a child?' But looking forward soon creates a common purpose. If we assume that these first answers are not ends in themselves but means to an end and ask 'if each of your hopes was realized what difference would it make?', both parent and child will very often give a version of getting along better, less fights, more conversations, and more friendliness. Both want the same thing.

What if family members just argue?

A family would hardly be a family if its members didn't argue and given that they are unlikely to be getting on well, arguments in the therapy room are common. In a solution focused session, the therapist will mostly ignore the arguments, treating them like 'interference' on the radio. However, if the 'interference' prevents voices being heard and the therapist has found no way to contain the arguing, then it is probably best to compliment everyone for being brave enough to give it a go together and then see people separately or choose to work with the person most eager for change.

How can everyone have a voice?

As we have suggested, inviting a client to detail their preferred future seems to be associated with a greater likelihood of change. So if there are six family members in the room, how can each be given the time and space to detail their picture? In these circumstances, it may not be necessary. Imagine a family who each in their own and age-differentiated ways have expressed the hope that they can manage to get along better. The therapist can then start with the first family member and ask, 'tell me *two ways* that you will know that this family is getting along better' and then move on to the next and the next, tracking each in turn as the family begins to build a rich, detailed multi-perspectival picture of the family which they wish to build. Not all will agree with everything and yet there will always be a significant amount of overlap in their views.

What if one member of the family appears to be scapegoated, blamed by another for the problems?

Arguing with clients is the only researched predictor of failure in SFBT (Beyebach and Carranza 1997). Thus, if one person locates the need for change in another, then asking questions that make the picturing of the preferred future interactive, as in the previous chapter, is more likely to be useful. This helps by seeking out the client's positive intent: 'It sounds like you are really worried about your son and his future, so how will you know that things are moving forward in his life in a way that would help you to stop being so concerned?' 'And when he is responding differently what will he be noticing different about you?' Accepting and acknowledging the parental distress and offering a constructive framing is likely to open up possibilities.

74

Scales in family work

The most common 'family' scale is a version of 'We'd all get on together'. Inevitably, family members offer different ratings and the therapist will aim to avoid any argument about who is right and instead enquire from each person what it is that puts them that high or what is preventing them scoring lower. A useful tip when working with families is to add up all the 'scores' (or get a child to do it!) and take an *average*. 'So, on average this family thinks it's at a 4. What, on average, tells everyone that it's that high?'

Another issue relates to when parents have brought a child for 'treatment'. For them, the child is the cause of their problems and so they will tend to use the scale to rate the child, as in 'I'll give him a 2' (often lower than what the child will say). There may be no way around this, but if at all possible the therapist should, in constructing the family's preferred future, aim at a '10' that is inclusive of everyone, not just the child. For example, even when the issue is the child's behaviour at school, so that for the parents '10' would be about the *child* behaving better, the '10' should include the knock on effects on family life of that. So '10' will become the child behaving at school *and* the parents being happy. The aim is to try and include the parents 'in the solution'. In the same way, when family members are asked about moving up the scale, and a parent says that the child will do X or Y, then the therapist will accept that and ask: 'And what difference will that make to you/your relationship with them?'

75

Couples work

Couples work raises similar issues to family work and there are many ways to manage the therapeutic conversations. The simplest way is to treat it as two separate but interwoven sessions in the presence of the other partner (if the other partner is present, which is not necessary for an effective outcome). In the following example, Pete and Dan are close to breaking up but would prefer to stay together. Each has been asked 'what are your best hopes from this therapy?' and each has expressed a wish for the other to change. As usual, the differences such changes would make are identical: 'We would be able to get on like we used to'. This gives Pete, Dan, and the therapist a common purpose. In the following excerpt, Pete has been complaining about Dan's behaviour.

Therapist:	So I can imagine that if he was a bit less selfish and thought about you a bit more instead of taking you for granted, that would make quite a difference to your life?
Pete:	Of course.
Therapist:	So if he were to make those changes, how would he know that you were pleased? How would you respond differently to him?
Pete:	Well if he did – and I am not sure that I can imagine it – I would be less angry all the time.
Therapist:	What would you be instead?
Pete:	I'd be more pleasant – I'd ask him about his day – I would cook but I'd be pleased and happy to cook rather than . . .
Therapist:	And if you were pleasant, do you think that he would be pleased?
Pete:	Of course. He calls me a grumpy bastard all the time.

Therapist:	So how would he respond differently to you if he saw less of the 'grumpy bastard' and more of the pleasantness?
Pete:	Oh he'd talk more probably – he says that it's not worth talking to me since I always bite his head off.
Therapist:	And would you like to hear him talking more?
Pete:	Yes – I'm telling him all the time that he doesn't tell me anything.
Therapist:	So how would you respond to him if he was talking more?
Pete:	Maybe I'd do some of the things that he likes to do which I don't enjoy so much.
Therapist:	Such as?
Pete:	Maybe sit and watch the football with him.
Therapist:	What about you, Dan – what would be the first sign that Pete and you are getting on in the way you hope for?
Dan:	He wouldn't be so angry any more.
Therapist:	What would be the very first sign of that tomorrow morning if a change were to happen over night?
Dan:	He wouldn't yell if I was in the shower too long.
Therapist:	What would he do instead?
Dan:	It would be nice if he just asked politely.
Therapist:	How would you respond to that?
Dan:	I'd be surprised . . .
Therapist:	And?
Dan:	And I'd get a move on.
Therapist:	What difference might that make to Pete?
Dan:	There'd be some hot water left for him!
Therapist:	And what difference might this make to your thoughts about your relationship if a day began like this?
Dan:	A big difference. I'd begin to think it was worth fighting for.

Therapist: How would Pete know that you thought your relationship with him was worth fighting for?

The simple structure of this conversation is clear. The therapist interleaves the picture of change in such a way that after a while 'cause and effect' becomes blurred in a 'chicken and egg' manner. The question of who has to start the change is lost in the process and what becomes evident is that all that matters is that one member of the couple starts to 'do something different'.

76

In the school

A primary school teacher, adapting solution focused principles, asks his class to describe for him what kind of class they want and how they will know the class is at its best. He asks them to write their ideas on flipchart paper which is then hung on the walls. From all the ideas he helps the class establish goals for the term.

Another teacher when taking the register asks each child to score him or herself on a 1–10 'happiness scale'. She uses this not as an objective measure but as a way to note differences: a child who suddenly drops from his usual rating will be given a little extra attention. The ritual also raises the children's emotional awareness – a key factor in learning.

The head of Year 9 takes a group of the eight students he is most concerned about in terms of fulfilling their potential and they have weekly meetings to establish what they are hoping to achieve in school and what progress they are making. They use scales to plot their progress and to look at signs of moving on.

A newly appointed headteacher called in to tackle a failing school meets the staff for the first time and, after acknowledging their – and his – nervousness, starts by asking them to tell him about all the things they like about working in the school. Everyone starts to relax and an increasingly lengthy list is developed (Martin Brown, personal communication).

A year head also creates a 'positive gossip' forum in morning briefings so that teachers can share constructive things they have noticed about each other and about students (Donna Jones, personal communication).

A headteacher develops a scale with a primary age child that is based on the child's favourite to least favourite foods. No-one else has a clue when he says to the head 'I'm a garlic bread today sir!' or, with a big smile, 'it's pizza today!'

An educational psychologist uses solution focused ideas to help make meetings more constructive. For example, starting the meeting as follows:

> So, we are all here today to find a way forward for Jim . . .
> Everyone has read the background reports so we should all
> have a clear idea about how things got to where they are
> today. Perhaps we could start with finding out what has
> changed since the reports were written.
>
> (Harker 2001: 35)

Other educational psychologists see the value of solution focused ideas in their consultative work with teachers: 'Employing the assumptions of solution-focused thinking leads us into conversations about resources, goals and exceptions. The idea that change can occur is promoted through imagining . . . and experimenting' (Wagner and Gillies 2001: 153).

These are just some of the numerous ways that colleagues and associates have made use of the solution focused approach. In addition, there is a wealth of written material about solution focused work in schools, including: anti-bullying (Young 2009), consultation (Wagner and Gillies 2001), reading (Rhodes and Ajmal 1995), solution focused schools and teaching (Metcalf 2003; Mahlberg and Sjoblom 2004; Kelly *et al.* 2008), peer counselling (Hillel and Smith 2001), and counselling (Metcalf 2009).

77

Schools: individual work

In the bustling school environment, individual counselling or coaching sessions give students a precious space for calm reflection. SFBT offers an approach that fits perfectly with the requirement for a time-limited intervention where students don't have to feel obligated to attend more than they feel is necessary. We have found that half an hour is ample time for a session and the majority of students appreciate the experience and wish to return for follow-up sessions. Other members of staff can participate as appropriate, and group sessions can also be run (see Chapter 79).

At the outset, students have to be told about the limits to confidentiality. When a student disclosed that his mother had been beating him with a stick, he was reminded that the coach had to pass this information on. The student became angry, insisting that it was a private matter and in any case the beatings 'didn't hurt'. He eventually agreed to meet with another member of staff plus the coach.

When students are asked what their best hopes are from the work, a common first response is 'don't know'. If the student persists in this position, then asking what the referrer might want will sometimes open up the conversation. It is then important to find a way to link what the referrer wants with the hopes of the student.

When asked about his hopes for the session, Hamid gave a number of 'don't knows'. When asked what the referrer's hopes might be, he gave more 'don't knows' until the therapist asked, with a touch of surprise in his voice:

Counsellor:	So your form tutor wouldn't want to see any changes?
Hamid:	I don't think so . . . well, maybe.
Counsellor:	So if he did, what changes might he be looking for?

Hamid:	I don't know.
Counsellor:	Would it be in the classroom, the corridor, the playground – where might he see them if there were some changes?
Hamid:	In the corridor.
Counsellor:	And what might he see you doing that was different?
Hamid:	Not running.
Counsellor:	What would you be doing instead?
Hamid:	Talking. I'd talk to friends and walk.

Hamid went on to describe having a better relationship with friends and being saved the aggravation of 'being in trouble'. These were outcomes he was willing to strive for even though to begin with the outcomes had been those desired by the school. In the end, as is usually the case in successful school counselling, both the student and the school were beneficiaries.

It is common for students to say *others* should change and agree to what they want. It is best not to get into discussion about how likely it is this will happen, even if the student is demanding the right to walk around their classroom whenever they want or to stay out all night. They know the rules, so there's no need to irritate them by reminding them. Instead, accept what they say they want and look for the *outcome*. In a case where a 14-year-old was blaming her teachers for all her problems, the coach (often a more acceptable title than counsellor or therapist!) asked:

Coach:	What difference would it make to you if they changed?
Jasmine:	I wouldn't be given detentions.
Coach:	What difference would that make to you?
Jasmine:	I wouldn't get into trouble.
Coach:	And what difference would that make?
Jasmine:	I'd be able to get on with the classwork.
Coach:	And if you could do that, how would that be good for you?
Jasmine:	It would make me happy.

Coach:	So if our work together leads to you getting on with your classwork and being happy, that would mean we'd done a good job here?
Jasmine:	Yes.
Coach:	What difference would it make to your mum and dad if that were to happen?

Irrespective of the starting point – the school changing or Jasmine changing – as the interactional description unfolds, Jasmine's motivation and commitment to change grow. Later she reports a change in her teacher's behaviour.

78

Schools: the WOWW project

'What are we going to do about 8c?'

WOWW stands for 'Working On What Works', a title that Insoo Kim Berg gave to a project she developed with Lee and Maggie Shilts on working with classes (Berg and Shilts 2005; Shilts 2008). An observer (or 'coach') notes and reports back all that 'works' during a lesson. Observers might be non-teaching staff but teachers are also able to observe each other. It is not a method of inspection and the teachers who take part are volunteers.

The WOWW observers are introduced to the class (at the morning tutor group, for example) and the students are told they have been chosen for a special project in which certain lessons are to be observed. The impact of the project is enhanced by how 'special' it is made to feel for students, and that would include who is doing the introducing: a senior member of the management team is a boon.

At the first lesson, the observer explains that they will take notes throughout and in the last five minutes they will tell the class what they have written. This feedback must be genuine and sincere. It can be helpful to walk around the classroom as the lesson is in progress and ask students their names when a positive action has been noticed. When feedback is given at the end, students are pleased to hear their names used. Although the feedback is to the *students*, as this is about the class and not the teacher's methods, some teachers appreciate the observer saying something about what they liked about their teaching, and this can be done in front of the class or privately afterwards, depending on the teacher.

The observations continue, if possible twice each week, for several weeks; one teacher told us she thought about ten observations was advisable, even though in our projects we have been limited to four.

A meeting with relevant staff is held prior to the start, half-way through, and at the conclusion of the observation period to assess, usually with the use of scales, what difference the observations will make and have made to class performance. There is no doubt that these meetings are invaluable (one teacher described them as the most important part of the project for her, as they helped her to remember to focus on what works) especially when all staff can attend, as they encourage the development of constructive dialogues around a particular class, which previously might only have engendered negative comments.

Feedback from students and staff has demonstrated the benefits to the students in hearing about the constructive things they have been doing. To quote one Year 8 boy:

> Telling us what we done good that's like an achievement, saying you've achieved a lot, and people want to keep it up so that they can get more compliments, and the more compliments they get the better phone calls home they get . . . their parents are happy, they're happy, so it's actually made it a lot better, in school and out.

There is a greater group feeling in the class and a sense of responsibility towards peers.

Of course, it's not all sweetness and light. The observer has to remember the importance of noticing what works, even when everything seems to be going to pot. After one such disaster, the class was asked to guess how many positive behaviours he had noticed. Somebody said 'none'; the most that was expected was three. He had written down eight and read them out. The students were stunned.

Acknowledgement: With thanks to Yasmin Ajmal, who ran the project with us, and the staff and students at South Camden Community School.

79

Groupwork

The literature on solution focused groupwork is growing. Metcalf (1998), Lee *et al.* (2003), and Sharry (2007) are some of the main contributors.

The solution focused approach offers a structure that helps oil the wheels of even the most challenging groups. Groupwork is particularly interesting from a solution focused point of view, as it involves bringing together people who may have little in common other than a problem. Clients are often interested in the experiences that others are having with similar issues, and so there can be a tendency for the group to become a place to share their problem experiences. It is not surprising, therefore, that the solution focused practitioner has to develop effective ways of guiding the conversation towards hoped-for outcomes.

The usual solution focused questions are employed straightforwardly. In the first meeting, all the participants are asked what their hopes are from the meetings, and then they are each invited to describe their preferred future, and subsequently to scale their progress. This may be done in the whole group if small enough or in subgroups if there are many participants. Subsequent meetings are used to explore progress ('what's been better?'), scale developments, and to use coping questions where there have been setbacks.

A significant difference between groupwork and other solution focused conversations is in the attention paid to what happens between people in the group. With individuals and families, each person answers the therapist's questions: the answers hold the therapeutic content and it is assumed that after family members leave they, in their own way, process what each has said. Groups do this processing during their meetings, so part of the therapeutic content is in what they say to each other – a burden shared is a burden halved is the usual belief. The solution focused mantra would be that a success shared is a success tripled and without diminishing freedom of expression and without ignoring difficulties, it is the solution focused group worker's task to direct conversations toward hopes and achievement. Once the group begins to experience the value of outcome focused conversations, they are as likely to put a limit on 'problem talk' as the therapist.

Certain rituals help (just as they help any meeting), such as 'let's go round and each take a turn to say one thing they've done in the last week they're pleased with' . . . 'Let's have two more turns'. By this time group members are likely to want to ask each other questions and while the discussion centres on achievement, the therapist can take a back seat.

Scales provide another structure. In some groups, everyone will have their personal scale allowing each person to be asked where they are and what puts them there rather than lower. Again, several rounds of this are likely to promote more 'free' conversation.

And at all times the group facilitator must keep in mind and constantly acknowledge the extreme difficulties with which many group members will be struggling. A structured 'setback' round can be a powerful route to constructive dialogue as it allows for the expression of a problem, something group members will expect as part of the process. With the problem 'in the room' each person can begin to describe their effective (and safe) strategies for coping or 'hanging on', the constructive things they have continued to do despite the influence of the problem, and the possible first signs that they are coming through the crisis. The subsequent conversation will sometimes leave the therapist with little to do.

The presence of so many potential co-therapists is what can make groupwork so effective. When clients are self-critical or stuck for answers, other participants are often ready to encourage and advise. This is not always welcome to certain individuals and we have found it necessary at times to coach group members to ask each other questions rather than to make statements. Similarly, we encourage participants to compliment each other.

Part 14

WORK
WITH ADULTS

A great deal of BRIEF's work is with adults, as will be apparent in the main body of the book. This section, therefore, looks mainly at the more 'marginalized' – those less likely to be referred for therapy. The clients described have been an inspiration to us and though we are not always successful, it is these clients who taught us never not to try. For further descriptions of inspirational clients, see Iveson (2001).

Homelessness

When we began our first experimentations with SFBT, we wished to test it to its limits. We asked our colleagues to refer clients who might not usually be thought of as candidates for therapy and some colleagues were adventurous enough to comply.

People with learning difficulties, the 'chronically mentally ill', and people with Alzheimer's were among those to come forward. We were not surprised that we were able to achieve good outcomes: once attention shifts from 'solving a problem' to improving wellbeing and quality of life, anyone can be helped. Any client who wants something different in their lives, even peace from the interventions of professionals, can, in theory, be helped towards making changes for the better.

This robust testing of the limits has been a continuing theme of BRIEF's work and as a result no potential client will be turned down on the basis of his or her presenting problem. This and the next five chapters will describe some of this work.

Jimmy was referred by an outreach worker for a charity helping homeless alcoholics. He arrived for his first session very drunk and very angry. For most of the hour he ranted about the iniquities he had suffered throughout his life, which had included extensive periods in prison and psychiatric hospitals. Unless safety is an issue, a solution focused therapist will politely ignore behaviour that is not conducive to the therapeutic process and do his best to stick with the questions that are likely to produce helpful answers. Eventually, Jimmy said what he hoped for was to have his own flat, which led to another rant about the futility of such a hope. It was after several more alcohol-fuelled rants that Jimmy finally gave his first answer to the question: 'Let's imagine that when you wake up tomorrow morning your life begins to move in the direction of getting a flat; what's the first thing you'll notice different?' There were at most no more than ten minutes of coherent responses to the therapist's questions but put together they described waking up in a doorway and instead of thinking where to get a 'drink', Jimmy would think of where to get a cup of tea. It would probably be from a sympathetic café owner he knew and the owner would see him early (so as not to put off other customers) and he would be polite.

At the second session a month later, Jimmy was even more drunk and angry. He had been offered a housing association bedsit of his own but had been denied the necessary benefits to enable him to accept. There were probably less than five minutes of coherence threaded throughout Jimmy's drunken ranting. But in response to the questions 'What sort of man did the housing officer meet that led him to offer Jimmy such a scarce resource?' and 'What was it about Jimmy that led this professional to choose him rather than any of the dozens of equally needing men and women?', it became apparent that Jimmy had attended his interview sober and dressed in clean clothes. How did he do this? Three months later the referrer reported that Jimmy had sorted out his benefit, had moved into a bedsit, and though it was early days all the indications were that he would make a responsible tenant.

The message is don't give up on clients before you even try.

Alzheimer's

Martha was brought by her daughter Ruth for counselling on the advice of a community occupational therapist. Ruth had initially asked for residential care for her mother who suffered from Alzheimer's and whose demands she was no longer able to bear. Martha had once been a prominent member of the community and spoke coherently about the advice centre she had set up and managed. Ruth said that it was her mother's more immediate memories that were lacking. However, when asked a 'Miracle Question', which gave her back all her *available* memory, Martha was able to describe everything that she and her daughter were planning for tomorrow (they were going Christmas shopping). Ruth was astounded. Other things were also discussed: how Ruth coped with the stress, how Martha managed to keep herself safe, how they could still have good times together, and how they had always had a close and mutually loving relationship. Ruth cancelled the second session saying that she wasn't sure if her mother's memory had improved but it no longer seemed to be a problem. Five years later, the therapist was invited to an anniversary celebration of the advice centre where Martha was the guest of honour. There was no hint of the Alzheimer's, although Ruth said her mother would have no recollection of the event the next day. Martha had found a way to live in the moment and enjoy herself and Ruth had continued to find looking after her mother more a source of joy rather than stress.

Eileen was also brought by a desperate daughter. A large and normally amiable woman, Eileen had suddenly taken to outbursts of violence. She had already lost one day centre place and if she was banned from another her daughter would have to give up work. Eileen spent the session either treating the therapist as a long-loved family friend or as an arch enemy to be whipped, with sudden bouts of sleep in between. When he could the therapist enquired about her good humour, her physical strength, the closeness of her family, and while she slept he asked her daughter how she coped and what differences she hoped to see in her mother if this meeting were to prove useful. Like many solution focused sessions in these often complex and uncharted waters, there was little that was recognizably 'textbook' in the session. To an outsider, and possibly even to the daughter, it would have sounded more like social talking. Nonetheless, the therapist was keeping in mind the hoped-for outcome and the present and past circumstances that supported it. It proved to be a single and inconclusive session but two years later the therapist received feedback that Eileen had experienced no more violent outbursts.

These were both desperate cases and ones that could easily have led to significant expenditure in an attempt to make up the deficits associated with Alzheimer's. In both cases, the families were able, and happily so, to continue without extra help.

82

Learning difficulties

As with children, the therapist's language needs to be adapted for clients with learning difficulties (for more on work in this area, see Bliss and Edmonds 2008). There is a tendency for therapists to applaud articulacy when all they are doing is to applaud their own form of articulacy. It is perhaps more useful to see our clients as possessing different articulacies or forms of language and to make it our task to speak as closely as possible the language of each client. This can be a struggle, especially when the therapist is not familiar with a client's way of understanding but patient trial and error will soon show the way.

A rough guide to communicating with people with learning difficulties is to be acutely aware of their responses to future focused questions. Abstract concepts can be difficult for some clients. This does not mean an attempt should not be made; we should not assume our clients have limitations, otherwise we come to impose them ourselves. As with smaller children, 'what are your best hopes from this therapy?' is too abstract for some and a more concrete path to a contract needs to be found, such as starting with the complaint. It is very likely that significant difficulties, mostly perceived by others, have brought the client to therapy. It is also likely that the client's position within these difficulties is not a happy one. Once again, establishing a simple outcome such as 'being happier' indicates the therapist's good intentions.

In the case of Margaret, a 50-year-old woman with Down's syndrome, not even 'being happier' could be agreed. Margaret had lived most of her life in a large hospital, initially for 'cretins' later for 'subnormals' and latterly for 'the learning disabled'. The hospital had been demolished and Margaret rehoused in a supported bedsit on a run-down estate. She was not happy. She fought with other residents (who had also been rehoused from the hospital), refused to cooperate with professionals, and was frequently attacked on the estate. The referral for brief therapy was a huge act of faith on the part of the community nurse who also taught Margaret how to get herself to the clinic. She came laden with bags and refused to say anything until she had a cup of tea in her hand. When she had finished it she left. Margaret was seen once every three months for three years. From the first session her behaviour calmed down, she began to look after herself, be friendly to her neighbours, enjoy professional contact, and become a 'character' on the estate. Fortunately, solution focused brief therapists do not go in for explanations because this outcome would have challenged the most inventive.

For three years the therapist made Margaret the hottest cup of tea in the clinic's largest mug and asked Margaret for a step-by-step account of her journey to the clinic. At each visit she recounted in a flat voice the most recent of her Homeric journeys. If she had seen her sister recently she permitted a few questions on what she liked about her visits, usually leading to a description of Sunday lunch, but apart from this and once a year a question or two about her annual holiday in Swanage, any question about the future drove Margaret into a mixture of rage and panic requiring a great deal of apologetic soothing. Once her mug was empty, Margaret would rummage in her many bags and produce a bright red diary. She and the therapist would count out thirteen weeks and Margaret would write his name, taught to her by the community nurse, on the chosen day.

83

Substance misuse

Traditional work in this field has emphasized the degree of 'denial' on the part of clients and the need for the therapist to challenge this. It is often assumed that treatment will be lengthy and that relapse will happen in virtually every case. From this perspective, SFBT shouldn't work – and yet outcome studies have shown it to be particularly effective in this field (see Chapter 12).

In SFBT, clients who are thought to be 'in denial' are not challenged but are asked about what they and others are hoping to see that will be different. If they don't wish to address their drug use, what else would they want to see different? If they answer with practical concerns such as housing, then this too is addressed, although if their lifestyle is likely to create problems for them in maintaining a tenancy, then they will be asked about how they would like to tackle things in future so that they can preserve their home. If they have already been rehoused and there are continuing problems, then what would others (including housing officers) wish to see?

SFBT would suggest that change can start from anywhere in a client's life and not have to be focused on the presenting problem of the substance use. A client who had been brought by his psychiatric nurse said that in moving up his scale he would stop doing crack and heroin but, 'I won't lie to you, I don't want to stop the marijuana'. Up until then he hadn't mentioned drug use to the therapist. It made most sense to focus on *smaller* signs of progress, rather than trying to deal with drug use of this magnitude and so the conversation continued to focus on the client getting out more often, talking to people more, trying to get more work, and so forth.

The assumption made in SFBT, as with all presenting problems, is that clients with addictive behaviours know what they have to do even if they don't initially know that they do: there are always 'exceptions', times that they are using less or not at all. de Shazer introduced the idea of asking clients to look out for and to talk about times when they 'overcome the temptation or urge' to use drugs (or other compulsive behaviours) (de Shazer 1985: 132). This acknowledges the craving that clients feel and lets them consider how they handle it. Some clients will downplay any exceptions, saying for example that on the occasion they didn't use drugs they had run out of money – but once reminded that that hadn't stopped them at other times, they can go on to examine their strengths in dealing with their strong urges. It is important to acknowledge the hard work involved in beating the symptoms of withdrawal. This is where *coping* questions are useful, in revealing the client's own skills in managing. One client was shaking when her session began, so strong were her cravings. As the conversation continued she began to become more composed and this seemed to be an 'exception' happening there and then. Another client spoke about how just being in the session was beneficial, 'otherwise I'd be out there right now trying to score'. Obviously some clients find the challenge to get clean while in their own environment too challenging and require a residential placement.

Inevitably, 'relapse management' is often an important element in treatment. Relapse doesn't mean that things are back to square one, as there was the period of abstinence or control that preceded it. How the client managed to control drinking as long as they did, and how they might pull out of a relapse in future, are discussed in detail.

Confidence scales are useful, as is an unusual task that de Shazer designed for clients who appear to find it difficult to say how it is they have good days:

> asking a client 'to each day predict whether you will over-come the urge to do coke the following day and then, at the end of the day see if your prediction turned out right, and then, account for how your prediction turned out right or wrong' most frequently will lead to a reported increase in the client's overcoming the urge to do coke.

> (de Shazer 1991: 88)

84

Mental health

de Shazer (1998) wrote that the practice of solution focused therapy involves us in 'radical acceptance'. Nowhere is this clearer than in working with people with mental health issues. In solution focused practice, the client's frame of reference is not challenged, however apparently deluded their framing may appear. de Shazer gave the example of a woman who believed that the reason she couldn't sleep at night was because a 'sneaky' neighbour had a machine that he used to beam rays at her bed (de Shazer 1995). When discussing this interview, de Shazer would make the point that there would have been no point in using words like 'it *seems* to you that he's doing this'. For her it was a reality and any hint of challenge by the therapist would have only led to antagonism and lack of cooperation. In the end, their conversation, concentrating on her need to sleep, led her to come up with the idea to move her bed. In a case where a client complained that the voices she was hearing were affecting her ability to get on with her daily life and she feared she would have to go back into hospital, de Shazer merely focused on the times she *did* get on with her life, so that she was able to recall and to amplify her own skills (de Shazer 1988: 140).

BRIEF has been asked to see a number of hospitalized patients on 'suicide watch'. On one occasion, the client said that the first sign of a 'miracle' happening overnight would be that when she woke in the morning, she would look in the mirror, see that she no longer had any facial hair, and would then check herself out of the hospital. The therapist asked her to go back to before she looked in the mirror and to consider the differences she would notice in herself then. She talked about feeling happier, and this led to discussion about what other patients and staff would notice about her, and subsequently she was asked to rate her progress on a scale. Although she became tearful in the course of the interview, the psychiatrist who was present said afterwards that this was the first occasion she had stayed for more than a few minutes in a 'therapeutic' conversation. She was discharged three weeks later.

On another occasion, a member of the team was working at his desk when a colleague entered the room with a client to check his diary to make the next appointment. The therapist and client finished up and shook hands, and the team member was to look on astonished as his colleague said to the client, 'it was a pleasure to meet you *both*'. It transpired that the client, who believed that another 'self' was advising him to kill himself, had consented to the therapist interviewing that other self about her intentions for the client, and this had helped the client connect with this self in an entirely different way.

In keeping with this spirit of acceptance is the question of the client's attitude to what treatment is best for them, and how they cope. One client diagnosed as paranoid schizophrenic said, 'I have to learn to manage my illness better', as he didn't expect to be 'cured'. Another client, living with bipolar disorder, had had to stop taking lithium when medical tests showed damage to her liver. She came for therapy feeling that her life was becoming chaotic. Using the conversations helped her to gain greater control in her life, but her belief that medication was essential to her wellbeing wasn't shaken, and as her new medication began, in her opinion, to take effect it helped to consolidate the control she had already achieved.

Clients who are asking to be given medication can be asked how they would know it was working, and how they might help it 'to do its job'. If the client answers by talking about a reduction in symptoms, he can be asked what he would want to see take the place of the symptoms. It may not be necessary for a doctor to take a position on whether the client should or shouldn't take the medication, although obviously they will talk with the client about dosage sizes and side-effects.

85

Trauma and abuse

Trauma and especially childhood sexual abuse are often thought to require long-term intensive therapy involving re-experiencing past events to come to terms with them. Once again, SFBT turns out to be as effective here as elsewhere (Dolan 1991, 2000; O'Hanlon and Bertolino 1998).

Deborah had been severely abused by a family friend and had been unable to go out alone for many years. She specifically wanted to recount her experience to a therapist to obtain a professional view on what happened. She had never described it before. A solution focused therapist would not see this as focusing on the problem. The client, by talking in a way she hadn't done before, was doing something different and trying to make sense of her life. If she had never spoken about the abuse it might have been impossible for her to have a coherent view of it. Hearing the story through her own ears (and through what she imagined were the therapist's ears) led her to see that rather than a shameful experience, she had heroically protected even more vulnerable children from abuse. Her heroism was continuing. Having denied ever going out alone, Deborah admitted to going to work alone every morning. Unfortunately, each departure involved a forty-minute ritual of leaving her flat by stages. Every morning Deborah castigated herself for her stupidity. What she failed to see was her successful daily struggle to keep her life going in the face of real (despite being psychologically induced) fear. This was the first of five sessions in which Deborah reclaimed her independence and her future.

In some situations where the client expresses the wish to tell the story of their abuse, the therapist might ask the client how they will cope *while* they are doing the talking. Adopting the ideas of Yvonne Dolan, we have asked some clients to bring with them a 'safety object' (Dolan 1991) that they can hold when the experience becomes too upsetting. The therapist is mindful that talking can itself lead to such distress that they have a duty of care to the client after they leave the session. Dolan has asked clients to prepare a 'self care' list of the kinds of things that help them cope, and asks them where would be the best place to keep such a list so that it can be accessed when most needed – for example, in the drawer with the knives, for someone who self-harms.

A powerful method for working with survivors of abuse and trauma is the response-based approach of Allan Wade (1997). If the client is describing an incident where they were assaulted or abused, then instead of inviting the client to 'work through' their feelings at the time, they might be asked how they *responded* in their thoughts, feelings, and actions to the assault, to elicit the resources the client drew on to survive (Wade 1997). Deborah was able to recall how during her own abuse, she drew strength from knowing that she was keeping her younger sister and cousin safe. Another client, describing her terror in her bedroom (at the age of 8) hearing her father coming up the stairs, was asked how she responded and she said she shut the door. Of course, this was ineffectual as a means to prevent the abuse, but she realized how in her own way she had tried to protect herself.

Another client, Wendy, was on suicide watch in a locked ward. She said she had no hopes from the therapy session yet having agreed to it the therapist assumed that somewhere she would have a good reason. Wendy maintained that only the removal of her past could open up her future, but she agreed to answer some questions. The therapist asked: 'Let's suppose that tonight, while you are asleep, a miracle happens; it does not take away the past but it does stop the past messing with your future. What's the first thing you'd notice tomorrow that would tell you that you've got your future back?' Over the next half hour, Wendy described the following day and then moved on to the life she would hope for after discharge from hospital. Later, asked a scaling question where 10 stood for doing everything she had described in her 'miracle' and 0 doing none of it, she surprised herself and the therapist with the number 7. 'But it's not the real me' she said. 'Then who is it?' asked the therapist. Though only a single session, Wendy's long-term recovery began that day.

A common feature of client responses to a solution focused approach to past trauma is that they will often spontaneously begin to take the steps recommended in textbooks. However, different textbooks make different recommendations, which suggests they are right for some people and wrong for others. For example, as each client begins to get on with life, some will report deciding to confide in a friend and how helpful that had been; others report taking issue with the abuser or another family member; and others might say, 'I've spent half my life going over it in my head and now I've decided to put it to one side'. The message is obvious – when we help clients to get on with their lives, they spontaneously find their own way to make that happen.

Part 15

SUPERVISION, COACHING, AND ORGANIZATIONAL APPLICATIONS

86

Supervision

'If your client were here now, what would he say that you have done that's been useful to him?'

Solution focused clinical supervision is a straightforward adaptation of solution focused therapy: an outcome focused process of enablement rather than direction, building on success rather than correcting failure, and privileging the supervisee's knowledge rather than that of the supervisor. It is a process intended to empower each supervisee to develop his or her own skills rather than imparting those of the supervisor. This does not mean to say that supervisors abrogate their managerial or standard-maintaining role; this is an important part of any supervisor's responsibility even though it is most often not required.

Although outcome focused, solution focused supervision pays close attention to the past and, just as in the therapy, it is the successful past that is likely to provide the firmest foundation for a successful future. Supervision sessions will therefore often start with a recap of the supervisee's recent examples of good practice: anything, big or small that the supervisee is pleased to have done in relation to their work with clients. This is likely to raise the sense of possibility when the supervisor asks: 'So, what are your best hopes from this session?'

Supervision then focuses on the *work* with the client. This means restraining the supervisee from telling the 'story' about the client, as this is likely to be a story 'explaining' (and embedding) the problem. Instead, the supervisee will be invited to consider the client's strengths, resources, and achievements, to speculate on their future potential, and then examine closely the client–worker relationship most likely to fit with the hoped-for outcome. This will involve looking at what has worked so far, and how further progress might be identified not just from the supervisee's perspective but also from the supervisee's best assessment of the client's perspective, hence the question at the beginning of this section.

Outcome or preferred future questions might begin a description of possible improvement with a question like: 'If at your next meeting there was a breakthrough in your work, what might be the first sign of this happening?' The aim will be to elicit a detailed, concrete description of a successful therapeutic conversation from the point of view of each participant and paying close attention to their mutual influence on each other through a description of the interactions between them.

Scaling questions are also very productive in supervision. A typical 'review' scale would be one where 10 = the work is satisfactorily completed and 0 = the point of referral. 'Where would you say you are now?' 'What has been your contribution to reaching this point?' 'How will you know when you have risen one point higher?' The full potential of these questions is realized when the supervisee has to answer not only on his own behalf, but also has to consider what the client's answers are likely to be. These multi-perspectival descriptions are one of the most creative aspects of the solution focused approach.

Just as SFBT promotes hope and motivation in clients, solution focused supervision does the same for therapists. One of the big dangers for clients is to have a therapist who has lost hope in them, who has given up on the possibility that change is possible because such a therapist will not be able to promote change. This is far more likely to happen if the therapist's focus is on describing and analysing problem behaviours. When therapists are encouraged to look forward to outcomes and when these outcomes can be described in realistic and possible terms, they are likely to keep their own hopes alive and be unafraid of 'difficult' cases.

87

Team supervision

Solution focused team supervision is particularly rich in possibilities. It will most likely begin by each member reporting on their own good practice and then commenting on an example of good practice elsewhere in the team. Creating a discipline of appreciation for specific contributions to the team's work will add to the team's confidence, level of performance, and expectation of success, factors clearly associated with job satisfaction and retention of staff.

In one example, the team of social workers had become so used to the routine of beginning the session with reports of good practice that two team members who had been co-working a particularly difficult family case came to the meeting with a specially prepared handout of the work they had done! It was noticeable that later on in the meeting, when discussion of the ongoing work of other members of the team began, others would say that hearing the presentation by their colleagues had already given them ideas as to what to do with their own cases.

The team can also be used as a resource, practising interviewing techniques together, role-playing future sessions with clients, and contributing to each other's professional development.

Two examples will convey something of the range of possibilities with team supervision.

Example 1: The Solution Focused Reflecting Team model

This is a structured approach consisting of five specific stages (Norman 2003):

1. *Presenting*, in which the therapist presents the bare bones of the case.
2. *Clarifying*, where the team asks questions.
3. *Affirming*, when team members compliment the presenter on his or her work.

4. *Reflecting*, where team members can offer ideas.
5. *Responding*, when the presenter has the final word.

Obviously, this can be a little time-consuming: it is usual to give thirty minutes to the process. Each of the stages is given a specific time allocation, and someone (the 'time monitor'!) will have the job of ensuring that order is kept. Of course, this structure can be used even when the team is not practising solution focused therapy. If the team *is* solution focused in orientation, then someone can act as a 'solution focused monitor', ensuring that as much as possible solution focused questions are employed by everyone in the 'clarifying' stage.

Example 2: 'One question at a time'

- A team member wanting help before her next session with a client volunteers to 'be' the client and the team becomes the 'therapist'.
- The 'client' then responds to the opening question, 'What's better?'
- Once the team has heard the response, each member writes down what their next question would be if they were the therapist.
- When everyone has done this, the team discuss the relative possibilities with each question and either they or the 'client' decide which to go with.
- The agreed question is then asked and when the client responds, once again each team member writes down their own personal next question before discussing and choosing what it will be.

Although it is unlikely, given time constraints, that even as many as ten questions will be asked, this exercise is almost always hugely fruitful in generating hope, possibility, and inspiration.

Coaching

If coaching had not been invented, the combination of solution focused therapy and solution focused supervision would almost inevitably have led there. The process of helping a professional improve her performance need be no different to that of helping a psychiatric hospital patient improve his lifestyle. There are, however, three differences between coaching and therapy despite the very many similarities (Iveson *et al.* 2012). The similarities are that exactly the same conversational framework applies to both:

- What are your best hopes from this meeting?
- What will be different if these hopes are achieved?
- What are you already doing that might contribute to the realization of these hopes?

The differences are:

1. A coaching client is much more likely (though not always) to come with an outcome focused purpose, often an improvement to some aspect of performance. A therapy client, on the other hand, is more likely (though not always) to come with a problem to be resolved. In effect, this adds an extra question to the process of therapy: if the client's first answer is that a problem disappears (e.g. 'I wouldn't be depressed'), the additional question would be as to what would replace the problem, to which the client can give an outcome answer (e.g. 'I'd be able to get on with my life').

2. The second difference is one of power. A person presenting a problem puts himself in a vulnerable position and there are no grounds for assuming that therapists are any less prone to abusing power than the rest of the population. Coaching has a different ethos. The client is more likely to present

aspirations than problems and the relationship will be more akin to that with an accountant or lawyer than with a therapist or doctor. Putting one's mind or body in the hands of another is more of a risk than one's career or income.

3. Tied in with power is the third difference: responsibility. Question by question, and often answer by answer, there is little to distinguish between therapy and coaching if both are solution focused. There might even be identical hopes; most common for both is 'more confidence'. However, if a head teacher is seeking more confidence and it is not achieved, the continued absence of confidence is likely to be more of an irritation than a problem in her career. But an acutely depressed client who sees gaining more confidence as a way back into life will be in a very different position should the therapy fail.

Therapies based on 'expert knowledge' in which the therapist has a theoretical framework supposedly allowing him to 'know' what is wrong with the client and how to 'fix' it are more exercised by issues of power and responsibility. Therapists are required to receive therapy themselves both to 'know' themselves and to appreciate the power and responsibility issues from within. When the therapist 'knows best', the client needs to be relatively compliant to follow the therapist's lead. If the client isn't, the therapist can decline to take responsibility for any failure by passing it on to the client, describing them as unmotivated or resistant.

Coaching and solution focused brief therapy share a more humble role in relation to their clients: they will be more likely to assume that the client knows best and the task is simply to help the client marshal her own knowledge and clarify the purpose for which it is to be used. Coach and therapist will experience their clients as resourceful individuals equipped and able to make their own decisions and therefore be less tempted to use their position, however well intentioned, to intervene.

Mentoring

Mentoring presents something of a challenge to the solution focused practitioner, since mentors have more knowledge and experience than their mentees and are expected to *use* this knowledge rather than rely on the client's knowledge. However, the challenge, though more explicit with mentoring, exists equally for coaches and therapists either when the therapist or coach realizes that he has knowledge and experience relevant to the client's issue or when the client specifically asks for advice.

When faced with these situations the therapist, coach or mentor might decide to put aside solution focused practice and come out with straight advice: 'I think it is important to set a bedtime and then stick to it'. 'In my experience it is better to wait until you can present a definite proposal before opening up the consultation process with staff'. 'If you are being bullied you should always tell a teacher'.

The problem with direct advice is that it is very often not followed and the more the advice impinges on our sense of autonomy or even our sense of identity, the less likely we are to take it. A mother might be quite ready to accept the research-based advice that it is safest for her baby to sleep on its back but be less ready to accept the advice that it is better to let the baby cry than pick it up after bedtime. The latter advice impinges too much on the kind of relationship the mother wishes to have with her child and is likely to be accepted only by those it suits. As therapy, coaching, and mentoring are largely concerned with relationships, advice on how we get these right is rarely helpful. We might all agree on the value of respectfulness but how we actually 'do' respectfulness will be unique to each one of us.

There is, fortunately, some middle ground. At the more solution focused end a request for advice can lead to a description of what difference successful advice might make.

Therapist:	Let's say you get exactly the right advice and it works – what difference do you hope it would make?
Client:	A big difference – she'd start treating me with some respect.
Therapist:	What would be the first sign?
Client:	A 'good morning' would be a start. It's a good day if I get a grunt at the moment.
Therapist:	And if she said 'good morning' how might you respond?
Client:	I'd probably faint!
Therapist:	And then?
Client:	Say 'good morning' back.
Therapist:	Would you be pleased to find yourself saying 'good morning' back?
Client:	Of course!
Therapist:	How would she know?
Client:	I wouldn't be able to keep the smile off my face.

As the description develops, the client's sense of possibility is likely to increase and she is likely to hear herself say things she might do that could promote the desired changes in her daughter's behaviour. She will have given her own 'advice' and is thus more likely to take it.

At the less solution focused end of this middle ground the mentor might use her knowledge not to give direct advice but to help inform her questions:

What do you think will produce the most useful response to a consultation process: going in entirely open ended with no recommendations or to go in with a definite proposal but one that is still open to modification?

And in terms of giving yourself the best chance to leave school with good results, do you think it will be more useful to hit someone when they provoke you or to walk away? (What would the other boys notice about how you walked away which showed them you were doing it with strength rather than from fear?)

In these instances, the mentor/coach/therapist has valuable experience but holds back from denying the client's own knowledge and judgement. The experience is embedded in the question but the answer remains the client's.

An exciting development in schools is the setting up of *peer* mentoring schemes (Hillel and Smith 2001). Usually this takes the form of older students mentoring younger ones. There is often an issue for schools in how to 'sell' counselling to students who have been identified as being in need. Students fear they are being labelled as having something wrong with them when they are referred for individual work. However, they are often comfortable in having mentoring from a fellow student, someone who, by being closer in age, they regard as understanding their experiences better.

90

Team coaching

The model for team consultations follows that for families. Though not a rigid formula, it is likely to be the 'default' starting point. If the team is small enough, each member will be asked in turn about their best hopes for the team (or whatever issue is on the agenda), what the realization of these hopes would look like if they were in evidence the next morning, and what events in the recent past might provide evidence that the hoped-for outcome is one that is possible. When groups are too large for such an individual approach, a series of structured smaller group exercises would serve the same purpose. Each group might be asked to list twenty small signs of a 'miracle' in the first ten minutes of the next working day. The composite picture is likely to be one that most would agree to be desirable and, just as important, do-able.

An effective large group exercise is for each person to say one thing they appreciate about their organization. Where criticism and complaint have become the norm, this simple process can have a powerful effect.

But of all the solution focused tools, scales provide the most flexible and creative framework for team development. They can be used to address any aspect of the team's function or functioning, enabling individualized responses without fragmenting corporate identity. They also allow the extent of difficulties to be expressed clearly but in the form of a single number rather than a catalogue of criticism and, with their aspirational structure, 10 always representing a positive presence, they once again engender hope and possibility.

All these techniques and conversational frameworks can be used equally well with successful teams wanting to stay on top and with failing teams wanting to get back on track. With the former there may be more emphasis on past success, while the latter might wish to concentrate more on defining a more successful future but there are no hard rules.

In one team where many members were afraid to criticize for fear of reprisals, the consultant used many scales to cover the complex issues the team was needing to address but to protect those in fear of speaking their minds he asked each person to keep their actual number on each scale private. This was the only difference. The same questions were asked that would have been asked if the numbers were declared: 'What puts you at your chosen point rather than lower?' and 'If you moved up one point what would be different?' This allowed all team members equal space to speak safely, which in itself produced a significant increase in team members' perceived levels of safety and the beginnings of a virtuous cycle towards acceptable levels of performance.

Teams wishing to reduce and make better use of their meeting times will also find inspiration in a solution focused approach. Establishing an agreed outcome for a meeting will do a great deal to prevent wastage of time. At a case conference, for instance, enquiring as to each member's best hopes for the meeting might lead to an agreement that making a good decision on the knowledge available would be a desired outcome. Enquiring about what specific knowledge would be relevant is likely, in a child protection conference, to lead to three areas of knowledge: research information on risk and safety factors in child care, information about risk behaviour, and information about signs of safety. This might seem all too obvious but in practice meetings of any kind, a more than useful amount of time goes on exploring and expanding on problems rather than on resources and possibilities.

91

Leadership

The last twenty years have seen a marked shift in thinking regarding leadership. Post-heroic Leadership (Badarraco 2001), Quiet Leadership (Mintzberg 1999), and Shared Leadership are just three of the ideas that have appeared and have sought to recast the traditional view of what leadership means. The challenges of a fast-changing world where minute-by-minute adjustments in strategy are required are seen as too complex for the slower-moving, top-down, centralized style that had been seen as the norm in any well-regulated organization. This shift in thinking highlights the need for agility and responsiveness and for everyone in an organization to 'be a leader', to take responsibility.

Fredrickson's work and that of her collaborator Losada on the positive–negative affect ratio, work derived from the field of Positive Psychology and striving to outline the necessary conditions for people to 'thrive' in their lives rather than 'languish', has also pointed to the conditions for flexibility in the workplace. Losada and Heaphy (2004: 680), for example, write: 'Within business teams, higher levels of expressed positivity among group members have been linked to greater behavioural variability within moment-to-moment interactions as well as to long-range indicators of business success'. Greater expressed positivity, in other words, is associated with a greater likelihood of workers experimenting and trying new approaches, and a capacity to experiment has become a prerequisite for business survival and success.

Within this new context of thinking and challenge the solution focused approach is proving a useful tool for managers, drawn upon as a model of coaching (Iveson *et al.* 2012), as a basis for strategic planning, for conflict resolution, for team building, for chairing meetings, and for staff review and development. But above all, the approach is proving its worth as a structured rationale for managers to shift their patterns of attention and focus. The solution focused leader's careful attention to what reports are doing that is working, to success and its foundations, offers staff a model that invites them in their turn to watch for colleagues' stand-out achievements, however small they may be, and to comment on them. This shift of culture, moving away from a tendency towards problem-identifying and fault-finding, towards the public marking of contributions made to team performance, fits well with one of the core findings of the Gallup Organization (cited in Buckingham and Coffman 1999) whose research sought to determine the characteristics of high-performing teams. One of the most useful questions for identifying successful organizations was: 'In the last seven days have you received recognition or praise for good work?' A positive answer to this question in almost every case revealed not just an appreciative manager but a culture of mutual appreciation throughout the team.

Part 16

FREQUENTLY ASKED QUESTIONS

92

Isn't it just a positive approach?

SFBT is 100 per cent a positive approach but in the mathematical sense rather than the more commonly meant 'let's-look-on-the-bright-side'. This makes 'positive' a misleading description. Mathematically speaking, positive is the opposite of negative and refers to what *is* there rather than what *isn't*. It is no more positive than a taxi journey: 'Not the airport' is a poor instruction to a taxi driver who will need to ask, 'then where?' in order to commence the journey. This is not seen as positive, just practical. Mistaking this practical approach for 'positivity' is to misunderstand the solution focused process and, at best, embark, like Pollyanna, on a foolish project. At worst, a distressed client may well feel insulted by what appears to be an instruction to 'look on the bright side'.

SFBT relies directly on the creative power of conversation, the turn-taking mutually referential construction of something approaching a common understanding. New possibilities cannot be created by accumulating absences (I won't be depressed, anxious, alcoholic, etc.). These lead to an ever-widening void. They must be created by articulating the feelings, thoughts, and behaviours that replace that which is unwanted. Whatever mix of depression, anxiety, and alcoholism is concocted, albeit in their absent form, it is hard to see a useful result. Confidence, calmness, and self-discipline on the other hand make a force to be reckoned with: 'What difference would a little more calmness make to your self-discipline?' is the sort of question that begins to weave together what the client wants that could not happen without 'mathematical' positivity.

As clients describe futures to which they aspire, the therapist will move between descriptions of feelings, thoughts, and actions but always coming back to the actions. The description of actions serves to bring the feelings out into the open, they are the outward sign of inward strength and the currency by which feelings are mediated. These descriptions also serve as prompts for future actions. Just as negative feelings vary, with periods where they are worse and other times when they are better, the same is true of positive feelings. We might appear to be and often feel confident, but this positive feeling will be interspersed with occasions where the opposite is true. Even so, we do not appear very different, our periods of confidence have taught us how to behave confidently and we are usually able to replicate the behaviour even at times of lost confidence.

Susan had been on the verge of suicide for a week, phoning the community mental health crisis team and her therapist each day. Each day the therapist asked how she would know as she put the phone down that the call had been worthwhile and after between five and fifteen minutes she would answer with a practical step: 'I've got shopping to do so after I put the phone down I'll make a list'. When she arrived for her scheduled appointment, the therapist asked:

Therapist:	Susan, what has kept you on the side of life since yesterday afternoon when we spoke?
Susan:	I don't know. I really don't know. I just want to die. I can't go on like this.
Therapist:	So what did keep you on the side of life when you felt so strongly that you wanted to end it?
Susan:	I made myself go for a walk. But I felt so awful I couldn't stay out.
Therapist:	Okay, so you made yourself go out for a walk. What else?
Susan:	I thought of coming here.
Therapist:	What else?
Susan:	I went to bed early but that didn't help because I couldn't sleep, so I got up again and then I felt even worse.
Therapist:	So what kept you on the side of life?
Susan:	I don't know. I think I maybe haven't quite lost the will to live.
Therapist:	What did that enable you to do that you wouldn't have done without it?
Susan:	I don't know.

Therapist:	What do you think?
Susan:	I had a cup of tea.
Therapist:	You had a cup of tea?
Susan:	Yes. I wasn't going to. I was going to do it properly this time.
Therapist:	So how did you get yourself to have a cup of tea rather than do it properly?
Susan:	I got everything ready. Filled the bath, put the razor blades out, got the bottle of gin and I was getting into the bath and a little voice said 'put the kettle on – you don't have to wait for it to boil'. So I put the kettle on and the voice said 'you may as well wait till it boils, you don't have to make the tea', and then when it boiled it said 'you may as well fill the pot you don't even have to wait until it brews', but I did and next thing I'm pouring a cup and thinking it's a pity to waste it!

At her next appointment, Susan told the therapist she was very angry with him, saying 'if it wasn't for you I'd be dead and I'm really pissed off with you!' This seemed like good news to the therapist, who said so and asked why he was getting the blame. Susan said she had woken up one day feeling worse than ever and without the will to live. She had once again prepared the bath, blades, and gin but at the last minute decided to 'do' the will to live even though she didn't feel it. And once again she found herself having a cup of tea – the archetypal British response to crisis.

Solution focused brief therapists will explore positive feelings and discover the associated actions so these actions can be performed even when the feelings have disappeared for a while. And just as feelings tend to generate actions, the reverse is also true: positive actions can generate positive feelings.

93

Isn't it just papering over the cracks?

Problem focused psychotherapies have traditionally and typically been structured around a 'surface/depth' distinction that has been central to the therapist's process of conceptualization. The client's behaviours, those which are open to the public view, his anger perhaps or his misery, are thought of as surface manifestations of more complex dynamics which are hidden from view and which are normally assumed to be out of, or beyond, the awareness of the client. These depth processes have traditionally been seen as more important, and it is these processes that are brought into play in therapy through the expertise of the therapist who is trained to see through the surface manifestations. The therapist, in other words, is generally thought to be able to access a deeper level of psychological process and it is this level that is assumed to be 'causative' of the surface level phenomena. The presence of this distinction is evidenced in the language of the professional. Whenever the word 'symptom' is used in clinical discussions, it is an indicator of 'surface/depth' thinking as is the use in clinics of the phrase 'presenting problem'. The latter tends to be paired with an alternative problem formulation description often labelled 'underlying problem'. The client's knowledge is assumed through this choice of words to be superficial, the therapist's to be deeper – and 'deeper' knowledge is assumed to be of more value. Unless this hidden, 'depth' level is addressed, therapists propose, change will be short-lived, akin to 'papering over the cracks' or 'tidying the deck-chairs on the decks of the Titanic', activities framed as futile. It is on this basis that therapists have felt able to attack and condemn counsellors as 'not deep enough', and we have seen coaches desperate to garner the trappings of the therapists' societal kudos through their appropriation of the processes and practices of psychometric testing, their way of going beyond the client's knowledge and making clear to all that they have a knowledge base that is not open to all, and in particular is not open to the client.

What is important perhaps to recognize is that the 'surface/depth' distinction, although it has been immensely powerful across all the fields of western thinking, is just one way of understanding; it is merely a way of thinking, a metaphor, a way of making sense of our experiences and as with any metaphor its value lies not in its 'truth', since metaphors are not true or untrue, but in its utility. And if we consider utility we can think about that broadly within the treatment system. Is it useful to clients? What is its impact on them? Is it useful to therapists? It could, for example, be argued that one of the impacts of this particular metaphor has been its tendency to disempower the client and to enhance the status and position of the therapist in equal proportion. Even if the metaphor has provided a basis for effective treatments, and it surely has, its effects are not universally beneficial.

SFBT is based on an alternative proposition: people change when they shift their ways of describing their worlds and their experiences, when they move out of problem-talk and into solution-talk. The solution focused therapist therefore works hard to work with the client's account, striving to stay with the client rather than to peer beneath or beyond or to determine hypotheses of causation. And the research in the model shows that this alternative framing of the therapeutic process also provides a basis for effective therapy and long-lasting change. If we as therapists can determine that outcomes are good, then our choice of model, of 'metaphor', becomes in essence an aesthetic rather than a pragmatic question: 'What sort of way do I choose to think about the people that I work with, what sort of relationship do I want to develop with my clients, and which way of thinking is most likely to facilitate these outcomes'. Metaphors, we need to remember are merely metaphors, even though at times we forget that and treat them as if they are real, as if surface and depth really exist, rather than representing arbitrary (even if useful) distinctions that we create in our minds and institutionalize in our professional trainings.

94

It doesn't deal with emotions

'When you are feeling happy, what are you doing?'

This is the sort of question that critics use in arguing that solution focused therapists ignore emotions and feelings. There is an obvious response to this, in terms of outcome: if the client truly experienced the therapist as ignoring their feelings, the chances are that the therapy would fail; yet solution focus, as we have seen, has an evidence base. In actuality, in every solution focused interview the therapist will be heard repeatedly acknowledging the client's feelings ('it sounds like you've been having a tough time') and even on occasion directly asking about feelings, as in 'When you wake up tomorrow feeling happier, tell me more about what that feeling will be like for you?' However, it is true to say that the therapist will not 'deal' with emotions, instead moving swiftly to action talk.

In their article 'Emotions in solution-focused therapy', Miller and de Shazer (2000) use the philosophy of Wittgenstein to explain this emphasis on action talk. They develop the view that emotions can't be dealt with as separate facets of a person's experience; to do so is to reify an emotion as a thing, an 'engine' that drives them to behave in different ways. Clients will, for example, talk about how they lose control of their anger and therapists then engage them in 'anger management'. The authors urge us instead to see the client's feelings as related to the specific social context in which they are experienced. For example, if clients describe themselves as being 'angry' or 'depressed', the therapist's thought would be 'in what context are they angry/depressed and what would tell them things had improved in those situations?'

Therefore, while a problem focused approach is likely to focus on emotions that are presented as problems, such as anger and depression, the solution focused therapist will acknowledge how the person is feeling and then seek to develop a conversation that elicits emotions that are *resources* to the client, including optimism and self-confidence. The focus is always on the *doing* of emotions because, 'to paraphrase Wittgenstein, for us to talk about "inner processes", we need outward criteria that can be referenced by and shared with others' (Miller and de Shazer 2000).

Against this Eve Lipchik, one of the original Milwaukee team that developed SFBT, has stated, following the work of the biologist Maturana, that 'emotions are the basis of motivation, and motivation, rather than rational thinking, determines the decisions we make' (Lipchik *et al.* 2005: 59) and 'emotions can overwhelm rational thinking so quickly while rational thinking does not regulate emotions as easily' (Lipchik *et al.* 2005: 52). For her and her colleagues, there is a place for addressing emotions more deliberately than in traditional solution focused practice. For example, she states that

> neuroscientific developments . . . suggest that there may be situations where clients are unable, not unwilling, to collaborate productively. For example, they may not be able to access certain memories that could facilitate solutions because these memories are stored in a part of the brain that cannot be accessed cognitively . . . it is very challenging to explore possibilities of enhancing solution-focused work by learning about new ways to connect with clients, such as through emotions, and in nonverbal ways, including through the body.
>
> (Lipchik 2005: 69)

It might involve, for example, asking a client where they experience their emotions *in their body*. Working with a client who wants to diminish the control that anger has over her, the therapist might enquire what would take the place of anger; if she responds by saying 'peace and calm', the therapist might ask 'where in your body will you be experiencing peace and calm?' A further suggestion, based on views of how our brains 'learn', is that 'it may be useful for SF therapists to consider prescribing repetition of thoughts or behaviours that represent possible steps to solutions' (Lipchik *et al.* 2005: 63).

Interesting as Lipchik's ideas are, they are in danger of breaching one of SFBT's defining boundaries: the 'not knowing' stance of the therapist. The application of 'expert' knowledge, not shared by the client, changes the nature of the therapeutic encounter. It is not necessarily better or worse but it is different and the attention paid to neuroscientific theories will impact on attention paid to discovering the client's own way of knowing what is best.

However, neuroscience is still in its infancy and it is too early for us to know what will be the influence of ideas from neuroscience on SFBT – and, indeed, all methods of psychotherapy.

95

Isn't it just a strengths-based approach?

The mistake here is to see the identification of a client's strengths and resources as the primary purpose of the therapy, as if just the gathering of strengths will be sufficient to see clients on their way. Solution focused therapists are interested in a client's strengths and resources, but only those that might contribute to the desired outcome of therapy.

Josie:	I have been trying; I am slowly getting better.
Therapist:	What have you been doing?
Josie:	I've been trying to do things on my own, so I've started going for walks.
Therapist:	How did you get yourself to do that? We all know it's a good idea but when it's the last thing you want to do it takes enormous courage.
Josie:	I started off by borrowing a friend's dog for the day, so I had to go out.
Therapist:	That's very creative!
Josie:	[laugh] . . . I've done it a few times now.
Therapist:	How do you feel when you've done it?
Josie:	Fantastic, over the moon!
Therapist:	So how else has your courage and creativity helped you to get on with things on your own?
Josie:	I've been to the shop. Only across the road.
Therapist:	Roads can be very wide when you've been going through what you've been through; how did you do it?
Josie:	It's silly really, I talked to myself. I don't know what people thought but I said, 'Go to the gate, you can always turn back' and I just did it in stages, telling myself I could turn round and go back any time.

Therapist: So you found a way to keep yourself company! You're very creative, aren't you!

With more laughter Josie goes on to list several more creatively orchestrated acts of courage.

In this case, creativity and courage are 'strengths' identified by the therapist and gradually accepted by Josie. They are used in the service of her hope to 'get back to a normal life'. In a session with David, a shy stand-up comedian whose 'courage and creativity' at each performance was just a routine part of his job, these strengths would not have been pertinent; what he wanted was more confidence in one-to-one relationships with women. What turned out to be helpful here was to adapt his open, self-deprecatory style of humour to the more serious business of conversation. He didn't hide himself in his performances and discovered how not to hide himself in relationships.

Thus, the identification of strengths and other positive qualities in solution focused conversations is not an end in itself. Each 'strength' provides a way into a description of associated actions, any of which could be performed whether or not the client 'feels' the strength at the time. Like emotions or feelings, strengths are part of a client's hidden inner world and the solution focused therapist will be interested in helping the client identify how they manifest themselves in the tangible world. Negative feelings, especially those relating to problems, are acknowledged (in the same way as one would acknowledge such expressions socially) but not investigated. When Jack who wants to *stop* crying for his long-dead wife begins to cry in a session, the therapist acknowledges the hurt and moves on ('You've been hit hard by this . . . What do you hope might start to replace the crying?'). This is not to say that crying is in itself problematic. It is a perfectly positive and creative emotion and part of life, except when it gets in the way of living as it was doing with Jack.

96

What account does it take of culture?

SFBT is thriving in too many culturally diverse settings to be seen as culturally specific and because it deliberately lacks a psychological theory, it is a poor vehicle for cultural imperialism – requiring clients to adjust to the therapist's viewpoint rather than stick to their own. The opening question, 'What are your best hopes from our work together?' is also as close to a universally acceptable question as can be imagined. Since the answer to this question, and every other question, can only come from the client, it is the client who decides the session's content even though the therapist, through his questions, will be edging the conversation (but not the client) in a future focused direction.

Eve and her son Abram had been referred independently by mental health and children's services. Eve was coming to the end of a compulsory 28-day stay in psychiatric hospital having attacked her son one night and tried to strangle him. She was psychotic at the time and remained so for several days. She spoke no English and worked as a domestic in an African embassy. Abram, who was 14, attended school and spoke perfect English except in the session when he said nothing other than a polite hello and goodbye. The conversation was mediated through an interpreter who thought that the therapist's questions, especially the Miracle Question, were questions made especially for his 'country' – he thought they were fantastic. Much of the session was conducted through a drawing on a flipchart of a mountain with 'hospital' at the base and Eve's hoped for 'good health' at the peak: a scale detailing her achievements so far and the next possible small signs of progress.

Early in the second session at which Eve was reporting many positive changes, the therapist learned how to ask 'What else?' in Eve's own language. This caused great hilarity and a noticeable increase in her responsiveness. But not Abram's. By the third session (mostly a long series of 'what else' asked directly to Eve) she was well, settling into new accommodation and although Abram was still in foster care, he was home every day and there were no reported worries. Eve had been amazed at her treatment. She could hardly believe that it was all free and that she and her son had been looked after so well. She had lost her job at the embassy but they had helped her find and pay for her new flat. She had no idea why she had 'lost her mind' but had experienced warning signs for some weeks before hand. Now she knew where it could lead and that help could be instantly available she was certain that it would never go as far again.

Having found her own way forward (and hopefully the therapy was useful in this process) Eve, in the four-year follow-up (the interpreter had become a family friend and coincidentally met the therapist four years later) was well settled, spoke English, had a job, and had experienced no further psychiatric symptoms. Abram had moved back home for good, was finishing school and expected to go to university.

At no time in this work was any attempt made to understand what had gone wrong or explain it in cultural or any other terms. The therapist simply extended his trust to Eve in the same way as he would with any other client. He assumed that she was the best person to know how to resolve this difficulty and get on with her life and trusted that her answers, even though he could not understand them, would inform her of a viable way of living.

97

Isn't it just a form of problem-solving?

The answer to this question probably depends largely on who is asked it. If we approached most appreciative clients at the end of the work, they would be likely to agree with the proposition. Their experience would be that they came to the therapist bothered by a problem, probably not with a preferred future in mind or a pressing 'best hopes', and that during the course of the therapy they found a way of solving their difficulty. Most clients are relatively uninterested in the therapist's particular approach – merely in whether they achieve relief from their distress – and to the extent that they do achieve relief, then their problem is solved.

From a therapist's point of view, the difference between a 'problem-solving' and a 'solution-building' approach is considerable and is undoubtedly of significance; indeed, the extent of the significance is such that in the early days of the approach traditional therapists voiced the view that SFBT was inappropriate, if not unethical and possibly dangerous. They certainly did not view the approach as merely another 'problem-solving' modality. They focused on the clear and evident differences and asked how solution focused therapists could hope to bring about lasting change if they did not do what traditional therapists had always done, which was to deal with the problem.

At the heart of the solution focused approach is the invitation to the client to develop a detailed description of a picture of life when their best hopes from the therapy have been achieved and this picture is not determined by the problem that brought the client to therapy. There is, in this particular sense, no direct connection between the problem and the solution. A client coming to a therapist as a result of work stress and invited to note the days when she feels less stressed may notice that she feels better on those days when she takes a lunch-break rather than having lunch at her desk. A problem-solving approach would typically focus on the sources of stress in the client's life and invite the client to do something about them, whatever that something might be. The solution focused worker, however, might suggest that the client experiment with taking a lunch-break every day and watch out for what difference this makes. In other words, SFBT encourages the client to pay attention to those elements of their preferred future that are already in place and to do more of those things. This process is substantially and significantly different and deserves a different description in order to highlight that difference.

98

It's a formulaic approach

We would prefer to say that SFBT is a 'disciplined' approach. A well-defined structure to sessions helps us as practitioners to know our way around. There is so much to pay attention to in any given therapy session that having a tried-and-tested procedure makes a complicated task that much easier.

There is no denying that there are a number of apparently formulaic questions in the sense of questions that are often repeated and also questions that are used regularly session after session. The 'best hopes' question is used in every first session and others like 'what else?' are used repeatedly in every meeting. Each follow-up session begins with the question 'what's better?' and scale questions, for example, are deliberately employed in every session as a literal measure of progress. A comment by Nancy Kline is apposite: 'As long as the question generates new ideas, the question itself is new' (Kline 1999: 158).

In 1991, we invited Bill O'Hanlon to present on his model of solution oriented brief therapy for the first time. Although he talked at length about the use of future focused questions, he did not refer to the Miracle Question. When we asked him why not, he said 'I don't like using formulaic questions'. They cramped his style, he explained, saying that he favoured a more spontaneous style of responding in the moment to the client. Even Eve Lipchik, one of the founders of SFBT with de Shazer and Berg, has stated that 'I have come to value the theoretical underpinnings as much as, if not more than, the techniques' (Lipchik 2009: 60) and complained that it became increasingly 'formulaic in manner' the more it was presented and the essential techniques 'took on a life of their own'. She has 'come to the conclusion that if a therapist internalizes the assumptions then he or she will not feel at a loss about what question to ask next' (2009: 55).

We believe that there is enough of a range of different questions in the solution focused 'book' for us not to have to worry about becoming too rigid or predictable. There is, however, a serious point to be made here. In 1997, the *British Journal of Family Therapy* issued a special edition in which they published several outcome studies in SFBT. de Shazer and Berg contributed a short introductory paper in which they delineated four 'characteristic features' of SFBT, the first of which stated: 'At some point in the first interview, the therapist will ask the "Miracle Question"' (de Shazer and Berg 1997: 123). Formulaic, indeed! Their point, however, was that 'in a research context the model used must be apparent and clearly demonstrated' (ibid.). They went on to say 'Obviously, the presence of these characteristics says nothing whatsoever about the quality of the therapy' (ibid.) – the mere fact that someone asks the Miracle Question doesn't guarantee that they are doing a good job. But it is essential that 'the researcher is able to demonstrate that the model of therapy being tested is indeed the model used by the therapists. Otherwise any and all findings are suspect' (ibid.).

Learning a new approach is difficult. We would recommend that a beginner start by slavishly (rigidly, formulaically) following the structure of SFBT and *then*, after a few years of practice, they can start to improvise and, like O'Hanlon, find the style that suits them personally!

99

Can it be used with other approaches?

SFBT can be used alongside any other approach. However, it would be a mistake, we believe, to think that SFBT can be integrated with other approaches. Its distinctive philosophy and language means that when a problem focused approach is conducted and solution focused questions are added, it is as if the therapist is moving from a problem focus to a solution focus and back again. In other words, they are being *eclectic*, not *integrative*.

Solution focused questions can be incorporated by practitioners of other approaches and it would obviously be helpful to any therapeutic endeavour to use, for example, future focused questions to elicit client's hopes, and scale questions to examine the degree of progress they have made. In this sense, even if someone were psychodynamic in orientation – to take as an example the approach usually regarded as furthest from a brief therapy – they could make good use of solution focused questions.

A different question concerns which approaches might be regarded as closest to solution focus. Indeed, what approaches do solution focused practitioners themselves use when they're stuck or failing? Michael Hoyt, writing under the heading 'opening the lens', refers to clinicians borrowing from various models as being consistent with 'the solution focused metamessage "Do What Works"' but adds that 'all therapists, however, more or less think they "do what works" (why else would they do what they do?), so it seems reasonable to establish more specific criteria for what may be consistent with the spirit and intentions of solution focused intervention' (Hoyt 2009: 177–178). He draws in particular from Motivational Interviewing, Appreciative Inquiry, Narrative Therapy, and the MRI approach (the brief therapy forerunner to solution focus, in which he highlights 'go slow messages' and 'predicting setbacks' as key) for those competency based interventions and ideas he regards as being closest to SFBT (2009: 179–182). de Shazer, speaking at a conference at the MRI in 1994, which was attended by a member of BRIEF, said that when solution focus doesn't work, what he and his team do then 'looks very much like what they do here'.

Hoyt also says, of 'kindness, humour, faith, respect, and love', that

> these often assumed or taken-for-granted qualities provide for the soil in which various techniques may take root. Solution focused therapists operate from a deep, abiding belief that people, if treated right, are competent and capable. We are in search of *their* solutions and, while not always, I generally have found that the harder I listen, the smarter the client gets – often in ways that I would not have expected or imagined. This belief allows the solution focused therapist 'to look for the light instead of cursing the darkness'.

(Hoyt 2009: 181)

100

Self-help SFBT

Self-help books drawing on the solution focused approach abound (Weiner-Davis 1992, 2001; O'Hanlon and Hudson 1994; Miller and Berg 1995; O'Hanlon 1999; Metcalf 2004). The application is simple and straightforward and the challenge, as with all self-help texts is also clear – how to make oneself work hard enough in the absence of the other, usually a therapist or coach, whose persistence takes us beyond the point where left to our own devices we give up. In relation to any difficulty we can ask ourselves:

- How will I know that the problem is resolved?
- What 20 differences will that resolution lead to?
- What 20 ways will tell others that the problem is resolved?
- On a scale of 0 to 10 with 10 standing for complete resolution and 0 the opposite where am I now?
- What 10 things am I noticing that tell me that I am at that point and not lower?
- What 10 things are other people noticing?
- How will I and others notice that I have moved just one point up on the scale? Of all the things that will evidence one point up, which two would be the easiest for me to experiment with doing consistently for the next week and seeing what difference that will make to my life?

As we can see, the application of solution focused questions is simple. Take a useful exercise for New Year's Day. Imagine that it is December 31st, the end of the year, and as you look back over your year you realize that this is a year in which you have done yourself justice in every way.

- What will be telling you that this has been as good a year as you could have hoped for?

- What will be telling others that this has been a year of real progress for you?
- What will be the smallest signs that will tell you that progress is being made in the right direction?

And as you review your project each fortnight, a simple scale will help you to keep track of your progress.

Let's try just one more example. Bring to mind a relationship that you would dearly love to see improving in your life. Sit down with a piece of paper and describe twenty changes in the other person that would tell you that things were getting better between the two of you. Having completed that task, sit with your sheet of paper in front of you and read over your list at least once – take your time – imagining how pleased you would be to see these changes and how you would feel different towards the other person involved, how benevolent, how warm perhaps, how grateful and how appreciative. Having reflected on this change, take another piece of paper and make a list of forty ways that the other would notice the change in you – changes from the most obvious, the smile, the cup of tea, the 'good morning', to the more subtle – perhaps the way that you would talk about this person to mutual acquaintances. Re-read the list of changes that you have made and then tear up and throw away the first list, the description of changes in the other. For the next week, act as if the changes in the other have happened – watch out for what difference it makes.

The possibilities for solution focused self-help questions are endless. Good luck.

References

Andersen, T. (Ed.) (1990) *The Reflecting Team: Dialogue and Dialogues about the Dialogues.* Broadstairs, Kent: Borgmann.

Badarraco, J. (2001) We don't need another hero. *Harvard Business Review*, 79(8): 120–126.

Berg, I. K. (1991) *Family Preservation.* London: Brief Therapy Press.

Berg, I. K. and de Shazer, S. (1993) Making numbers talk: language in therapy. In S. Friedman (Ed.), *The New Language of Change: Constructive Collaboration in Psychotherapy.* New York: Guilford Press.

Berg, I. K. and Miller, S. (1992) *Working with the Problem Drinker: A Solution Focused Approach.* New York: W. W. Norton.

Berg, I. K. and Shilts, L. (2005) Keeping the solutions inside the classroom. *ASCA School Counselor*, July/August.

Berg, I. K. and Steiner, T. (2003) *Children's Solution Work.* New York: W. W. Norton.

Beyebach, M. and Carranza, V. E. (1997) Therapeutic interaction and dropout: measuring relational communication in solution-focused therapy. *Journal of Family Therapy*, 19: 173–212.

Bliss, E. V. and Edmonds, G. (2008) *A Self-determined Future with Asperger's Syndrome: Solution Focused Approaches.* London: Jessica Kingsley.

Buckingham, M. and Coffman, C. (1999) *First, Break All the Rules.* New York: Simon & Schuster.

Cade, B. (2007) Springs, streams and tributaries: a history of the brief, solution-focused approach. In T. Nelson and F. Thomas (Eds.), *Handbook of Solution-Focused Brief Therapy.* New York: Haworth.

Cockburn, J. T., Thomas, F. N. and Cockburn, O. J. (1997) Solution-focused therapy and psychosocial adjustment to orthopedic rehabilitation in a work hardening program. *Journal of Occupational Rehabilitation*, 7: 97–106.

DeJong, P. and Berg, I. K. (2008) *Interviewing for Solutions* (3rd edn.). Pacific Grove, CA: Brooks/Cole.

de Shazer, S. (1982) *Patterns of Brief Family Therapy*. New York: Guilford Press.

de Shazer, S. (1984) The death of resistance. *Family Process*, 23: 11–17.

de Shazer, S. (1985) *Keys to Solution in Brief Therapy*. New York: W. W. Norton.

de Shazer, S. (1987) Minimal elegance. *Family Therapy Networker*, 11: 57–60.

de Shazer, S. (1988) *Clues: Investigating Solutions in Brief Therapy*. New York: W. W. Norton.

de Shazer, S. (1989) Resistance revisited. *Contemporary Family Therapy*, 11: 227–233.

de Shazer, S. (1991) *Putting Difference to Work*. New York: W. W. Norton.

de Shazer, S. (1994) *Words were Originally Magic*. New York: W. W. Norton.

de Shazer, S. (1995) *Coming Through The Ceiling*. Training video (available at: www.sfbta.org).

de Shazer, S. (1998) *Radical acceptance* (accessed 20 February 1998 from website of BFTC).

de Shazer, S. (2001) Handout at presentation for BRIEF, entitled 'Conversations with Steve de Shazer'.

de Shazer, S. and Berg, I. K. (1997) 'What works?' Remarks on research aspects of solution-focused brief therapy. *Journal of Family Therapy*, 19: 121–124.

de Shazer, S. and Isebaert, L. (2003) The Bruges Model: a solution-focused approach to problem drinking. *Journal of Family Psychotherapy*, 14: 43–52.

de Shazer, S., Berg, I. K., Lipchik, L., Nunnally, E., Molnar, A., Gingerich, W. *et al.* (1986) Brief therapy: focused solution development. *Family Process*, 25: 207–222.

de Shazer, S., Dolan, Y., Korman, H., Trepper, T., McCollum, E. and Berg, I. K. (2007) *More than Miracles: The State of the Art of Solution-Focused Brief Therapy*. New York: Haworth.

Dolan, Y. (1991) *Resolving Sexual Abuse*. New York: W. W. Norton.

Dolan, Y. (2000) *Beyond Survival*. London: Brief Therapy Press.

Eakes, G., Walsh, S., Markowski, M., Cain, H. and Swanson, M. (1997) Family-centred brief solution-focused therapy with chronic schizophrenia: a pilot study. *Journal of Family Therapy*, 19: 145–158.

Franklin, C., Moore, K. and Hopson, L. (2008) Effectiveness of solution-focused brief therapy in a school setting. *Children and Schools*, 30: 15–26.

Freud, S. (1912) *The Dynamics of Transference*. Standard Edition, Vol. XII. London: The Hogarth Press.

George, E., Iveson, C. and Ratner, H. (1999) *Problem to Solution: Brief Therapy with Individuals and Families* (revised and expanded edition). London: Brief Therapy Press.

Gergen, K. J. (1999) *An Invitation to Social Construction*. London: Sage.

Haley, J. (1973) *Uncommon Therapy: The Psychiatric Techniques of Milton H. Erickson, M.D.* New York: W. W. Norton.

Harker, M. (2001) How to build solutions at meetings. In Y. Ajmal and I. Rees (Eds.), *Solutions in Schools*. London: Brief Therapy Press.

Herrero de Vega, M. (2006) Un estudio sobre el proceso de cambio terapéutico: el manejo de 'casos atascados' en terapia sistémica breve [A study of therapeutic change: handling 'stuck cases' in brief systemic therapy]. Unpublished doctoral dissertation, Department of Psychology, Pontifical University of Salamanca, Salamanca, Spain.

Hillel, V. and Smith, E. (2001) Empowering students to empower others. In Y. Ajmal and I. Rees (Eds.), *Solutions in Schools*. London: Brief Therapy Press.

Hoyt, M. H. (2009) *Brief Psychotherapies: Principles and Practices*. Phoenix, AZ: Zeig, Tucker & Theisen.

Iveson, C. (1994) *Preferred Futures – Exceptional Pasts*. Presentation to the European Brief Therapy Association Conference, Stockholm.

Iveson, C. (2001) *Whose Life? Working with Older People*. London: Brief Therapy Press.

Iveson, C., George, E. and Ratner, H. (2012) *Brief Coaching: A Solution Focused Approach*. London: Routledge

Kelly, M., Kim, J. and Franklin, C. (2008) *Solution Focused Brief Therapy in Schools: A 360-Degree View of Research and Practice*. Oxford: Oxford University Press.

Kline, N. (1999) *A Time to Think*. London: Cassell.

Korman, H. (2004) *The Common Project* (available at: www.sikt.nu).

Lee, M. Y. (1997) A study of solution-focused brief family therapy: outcomes and issues. *American Journal of Family Therapy*, 25: 3–17.

Lee, M. Y., Greene, G. J., Uken, A., Sebold, J. and Rheinsheld, J. (1997) Solution-focused brief group treatment: a viable modality for domestic violence offenders? *Journal of Collaborative Therapies*, IV: 10–17.

Lee, M. Y., Sebold, J. and Uken, A. (2003) *Solution-Focused Treatment of Domestic Violence Offenders*. New York: Oxford University Press.

Lethem, J. (1994) *Moved to Tears, Moved to Action: Brief Therapy with Women and Children*. London: Brief Therapy Press.

Lindforss, L. and Magnusson, D. (1997) Solution-focused therapy in prison. *Contemporary Family Therapy*, 19: 89–104.

Lipchik, E. (1986) The purposeful interview. *Journal of Strategic and Systemic Therapies*, 5(1/2): 88–99.

Lipchik, E. (2005) An interview with Eve Lipchik: expanding solution-focused thinking. *Journal of Systemic Therapies*, 24(1): 67–74.

Lipchik, E. (2009) A solution focused journey. In E. Connie and L. Metcalf (Eds.), *The Art of Solution Focused Therapy*. New York: Springer.

Lipchik, E., Becker, M., Brasher, B., Derks, J. and Volkmann, J. (2005) Neuroscience: a new direction for solution-focused thinkers? *Journal of Systemic Therapies*, 24(3): 49–69.

Littrell, J. M., Malia, J. A. and Vanderwood, M. (1995) Single-session brief counseling in a high school. *Journal of Counseling and Development*, 73: 451–458.

Losada, M. and Heaphy, E. (2004) The role of positivity and connectivity in the performance of business teams: a nonlinear dynamics model. *American Behavioral Scientist*, 47: 740–765.

Macdonald, A. (1997) Brief therapy in adult psychiatry: further outcomes. *Journal of Family Therapy*, 19: 213–222.

Macdonald, A. (2005) Brief therapy in adult psychiatry: results from 15 years of practice. *Journal of Family Therapy*, 27: 65–75.

Macdonald, A. (2011) Website of Alasdair Macdonald, keeping an up-to-date eye on all the research in the SFBT field (available at: www.solutionsdoc.co.uk/sft.html).

Mahlberg, K. and Sjoblom, M. (2004) *Solution Focused Education: For a Happier School* (available at: www.fkce.se).

McKergow, M. and Korman, H. (2009) In between – neither inside or outside: the radical simplicity of solution-focused brief therapy. *Journal of Systemic Therapies*, 28(2): 34–49.

Metcalf, L. (1998) *Solution Focused Group Therapy*. New York: Simon & Schuster.

Metcalf, L. (2003) *Teaching Towards Solutions: A Solution Focused Guide to Improving Student Behaviour, Grades, Parental Support and Staff Morale* (2nd edn.). Arlington, TX: Metcalf & Metcalf Family Clinic.

Metcalf, L. (2004) *The Miracle Question: Answer It and Change Your Life*. Carmarthen, Wales: Crown House Publishing.

Metcalf, L. (2009) *The Field Guide to Counselling Towards Solutions: The Solution Focused School*. San Francisco, CA: Jossey-Bass.

Miller, G. (1997) *Becoming Miracle Workers: Language and Meaning in Brief Therapy*. New York: Aldine de Gruyter.

Miller, G. and de Shazer, S. (1998) Have you heard the latest rumor about . . .? Solution-focused therapy as a rumor. *Family Process*, 37: 363–377.

Miller, G. and de Shazer, S. (2000) Emotions in solution-focused therapy: a re-examination. *Family Process*, 39: 5–23.

Miller, S. and Berg, I. K. (1995) *The Miracle Method: A Radically New Approach to Problem Drinking*. New York: W. W. Norton.

Mintzberg, H. (1999, Spring) Managing quietly. *Leader to Leader*, pp. 24–30.

Norman, H. (2003) Solution-focused reflecting team. In B. O'Connell and S. Palmer (Eds.), *Handbook of Solution-Focused Therapy*. London: Sage.

Norum, D. (2000) The family has the solution. *Journal of Systemic Therapies*, 19(1): 3–15.

Nunnally, E., de Shazer, S., Lipchik, E. and Berg, I. K. (1985) A study of change: therapeutic theory in process. In E. Efron (Ed.), *Journeys:*

Expansion of the Strategic-Systemic Therapies. New York: Brunner/ Mazel.

Nylund, D. and Corsiglia, V. (1994) Becoming solution-focused in brief therapy: remembering something important we already knew. *Journal of Systemic Therapies*, 13(1): 5–12.

O'Hanlon, B. (1999) *Do One Thing Different: And Other Uncommonly Simple Solutions to Life's Persistent Problems*. New York: Morrow.

O'Hanlon, B. and Beadle, S. (1996) *A Field Guide to PossibilityLand*. London: Brief Therapy Press.

O'Hanlon, B. and Bertolino, B. (1998) *Even from a Broken Web: Brief, Respectful Solution-Oriented Therapy for Sexual Abuse and Trauma*. New York: Wiley.

O'Hanlon, W. and Hudson, P. (1994) *Love is a Verb: How to Stop Analysing Your Relationship and Start Making it Great*. New York: W. W. Norton.

Perkins, R. (2006) *The effectiveness of one session of therapy using a single-session therapy approach for children and adolescents with mental health problems* (cited at www.solutionsdoc.co.uk).

Rhodes, J. and Ajmal, Y. (1995) *Solution Focused Thinking in Schools*. London: Brief Therapy Press.

Seidel, A. and Hedley, D. (2008) The use of solution-focused brief therapy with older adults in Mexico: a preliminary study. *American Journal of Family Therapy*, 36: 242–252.

Sharry, J. (2007) *Solution Focused Group Work* (2nd edn.). London: Sage.

Shennan, G. and Iveson, C. (2011) From solution to description: practice and research in tandem. In C. Franklin, T. S. Trepper, W. J. Gingerich and E. E. McCollum (Eds.), *Solution-focused Brief Therapy: A Handbook of Evidence-based Practice*. New York: Oxford University Press.

Shilts, L. (2008) The WOWW Program. In P. DeJong and I. K. Berg (Eds.), *Interviewing for Solutions* (3rd edn.). Pacific Grove, CA: Brooks/ Cole.

Simon, J. (2010) *Solution Focused Practice in End-of-Life and Grief Counseling*. New York: Springer.

Simon, J. and Nelson, T. (2007) *Solution Focused Brief Practice with Long Term Clients in Mental Health Services: 'I Am More Than My Label'*. New York: Haworth.

Sundman, P. (1997) Solution-focused ideas in social work. *Journal of Family Therapy*, 19: 159–172.

Tohn, S. L. and Oshlag, J. A. (1997) *Crossing the Bridge: Integrating Solution-Focused Therapy into Clinical Practice*. Sudbury, MA: Solutions Press.

Turnell, A. and Edwards, S. (1999) *Signs of Safety*. New York: W. W. Norton.

Wade, A. (1997) Small acts of living: everyday resistance to violence and other forms of oppression. *Contemporary Family Therapy*, 19: 23–39.

Wagner, P. and Gillies, E. (2001) Consultation: a solution-focused approach. In Y. Ajmal and I. Rees (Eds.), *Solutions in Schools.* London: Brief Therapy Press.

Walsh, T. (2010) *The Solution-Focused Helper.* London: McGraw-Hill.

Watzlawick, P., Weakland, J. and Fisch, R. (1974) *Change: Principles of Problem Formation and Problem Resolution.* New York: W. W. Norton.

Weakland, J., Fisch, R., Watzlawick, P. and Bodin, A. (1974) Brief therapy: focused problem resolution. *Family Process*, 13: 141–168.

Weiner-Davis, M. (1992) *Divorce Busting.* New York: Simon & Schuster.

Weiner-Davis, M. (2001) *The Divorce Remedy.* New York: Simon & Schuster.

Weiner-Davis, M., de Shazer, S. and Gingerich, W. (1987) Building on pretreatment change to construct the therapeutic solution: an exploratory study. *Journal of Family and Marital Therapy*, 13: 359–363.

Young, S. (2009) *Solution-Focused Schools: Anti-Bullying and Beyond.* London: Brief Therapy Press.

Zimmerman, T. S., Jacobsen, R. B., MacIntyre, M. and Watson, C. (1996) Solution-focused parenting groups: an empirical study. *Journal of Systemic Therapies*, 15: 12–25.

Zimmerman, T. S., Prest, L. A. and Wetzel, B. E. (1997) Solution-focused couples therapy groups: an empirical study. *Journal of Family Therapy*, 19: 125–144.